Audrey Ellis
COLOURFUL ENTERTAINING
Cooking for the Hostess

Hamlyn

London · New York · Sydney · Toronto

ACKNOWLEDGEMENTS
The author and publishers would like to thank the
following for their co-operation in supplying colour
photographs for this book:
Adams Foods Limited (Territorial
English Cheeses) page 1
Birds Eye Foods Limited page 50
Colmans Mustard page 110
Dutch Dairy Bureau pages 63 and 110
Mushroom Growers Association page 110
The Pastry Bureau page 20
Taunton Cider page 96
John West Foods Limited page 39

Published by
The Hamlyn Publishing Group Limited
London · New York · Sydney · Toronto
Astronaut House, Feltham, Middlesex, England
© Copyright The Hamlyn Publishing Group
Limited 1975
ISBN 0 600 31861 3
Phototypeset by Tradespools Limited, Frome, Somerset
Printed in England by Cox and Wyman Limited,
Fakenham and Reading

Line drawings by The Hayward Art Group
(Elaine Handley)

Introduction

Since we enjoy food as much with the eye as with the palate, its appearance is just as important as the way it tastes. Dreary looking food actually discourages appetite – the nutrition experts tell us so. Colourful food is appetising and the battle is half won before the first mouthful, each time you serve a meal with just the right attractive touches. Every eye round the table brightens, taste buds begin to tingle and the meal is off to a good start. Guests too are bound to be impressed when the food looks every bit as lovely as it tastes. With a little expertise in the art of garnishing, and a careful hand in balancing flavours and textures, you're well on the way to becoming an accomplished hostess. This book is packed not only with useful recipes but all sorts of hints on the successful presentation of food. The results reflect your enjoyment of the time spent preparing it.

For the whole effect of a table setting depends as much on the choice and arrangement of plates, glasses, tableware and even the colour of cloth and napkins, as on the food itself. Even if you have only one full set of china, you can vary the cloth, candles and flowers to give you many different table settings, always to suit the mood of the meal. For this reason, I have included three short sections on the arts of flower arranging, table decoration and setting generally, and the service of wine. This last subject is becoming more important in many homes since wine adds an agreeable festive touch and is no longer a rare luxury.

In using colour to aid your party plans there is no need to be extravagant. All the suggestions given here are easy to accomplish and even those which require the maximum care to achieve, still only take the minimum of time.

Some of the recipes may look and sound slightly unusual but a glance at the ingredients column, cooking time and method, all clearly picked out for your information, will reassure you that not one is either difficult or complicated to make.

This book is for every woman who would like to be proud of her cooking, and never find it a chore. All the recipes are easy and clear to follow, with lots of interesting tips. The results are guaranteed to look – well, good enough to eat! And I can wish you nothing more complimentary to your reputation as super cook and hostess, than exactly that.

Audrey Ellis

Light dishes to serve around the clock

Eating habits are definitely changing. Meal times are far more flexible than they used to be. Friends who cannot help arriving at odd times of the day might enjoy a light meal rather than coffee and biscuits. Although you would not dream of serving a steak and kidney pudding at 3 o'clock in the afternoon, you should not be at a loss for suitable ideas.

Very few people expect to eat a heavy meal twice daily. So many of us are overweight that guests particularly appreciate being offered an appetising light meal.

Salads can be filling and sustaining, and also look delicious, yet remain fairly low in their calorie count. A tactful menu for diet-conscious guests might be a clear soup followed by one of the attractive salads featured in this chapter. Canned consommé is a great standby but you can always make your own clear soup with strong stock from a couple of beef or chicken cubes. Frozen green peas, finely chopped spring onions, sliced mushrooms and a spoonful of tiny pasta shapes all cook in the boiling stock in about 10 minutes, while the table is being laid and the salad prepared. If there is more time, savoury flans can be accompanied by a simple classic salad. Zip up the dressing a little to make it rather special. Two tablespoons of French dressing beaten into half a carton of natural yogurt, makes a creamy dressing with a pleasant tang. Or, if you want to offer a salady starter, chopped watercress or chicory looks tempting, tossed with a few chopped walnuts or peanuts in natural yogurt seasoned with salt and pepper, garnished with tomato slices or sprinkled with paprika.

Eggs have always been a good choice for meals; try Tarama egg salad or Mexicali eggs.

Fruit mousses also make good use of eggs, and although we are used to the conventional lemon or orange mousse, there are less obvious variations. Canned apricots and mandarins combine their perfumed flavours with eggs, cream and gelatine to make a more exotic version. Simpler still, a fruit jelly set to the syrupy stage and whisked into thick foamy evaporated milk produces a very delicately flavoured fruit cream. I add a few drops of lemon juice when whipping up the milk to make it thick and increase the bulk, which has the dual effect of quick thickening action and counters the unmistakable flavour of the milk itself. For family meals, this fruit cream is fine as it is, but for entertaining I like to fold in pieces of canned or fresh fruit, chopped almonds and glacé cherries, or layer the mixture over a base of sultanas soaked in sherry to plump them.

A joint of cooked ham in the house is the source of many light dishes. A can of ham in the store cupboard is an insurance against unexpected guests preferring a hot light meal. Slice the ham fairly thickly. Make up a chicken or beef stock cube with only ½ pint (3 dl., 1¼ cups) of water, thicken with gravy powder and stir in a couple of tablespoons of port, Madeira or sherry. Carefully arrange the ham slices in the sauce to heat through and serve with creamy mashed potato or savoury rice – both could come from a packet.

Frozen spinach makes an ideal second vegetable if zipped up by a spoonful of cream, a touch of nutmeg and, if you have it to spare, a well beaten egg white at the last moment.

Spicy pineapple glazed ham (page 13) and orange summer soufflé (page 19).

Tarama egg salad

Preparation time 20 minutes
Serves 4

IMPERIAL/METRIC	AMERICAN
8 hard-boiled eggs	8 hard-cooked eggs
2 oz./50 g. smoked cod's roe	2 oz. smoked cod's roe
small knob butter	small knob butter
2 tablespoons mayonnaise	3 tablespoons mayonnaise
salt and pepper to taste	salt and pepper to taste
½ cucumber	½ cucumber
1 lettuce heart, quartered	1 lettuce heart, quartered

Cool the eggs under running water and shell them. Slice in half across and scoop out the yolks carefully without damaging the whites. Cut a sliver from each rounded side so that the egg white 'cups' will stand firmly. Cover the egg whites with cold water until required.

Pound the cod's roe until smooth and gradually work in the yolks, butter and mayonnaise. Taste the mixture and adjust seasoning. Place the mixture in a piping bag with a large star nozzle. Drain the 'cups' on absorbent kitchen paper and into each one pipe a large rosette of filling. Make ⅛-inch (0·25-cm.) incisions lengthwise in the skin of the cucumber with a sharp pointed knife. Remove alternate strips of skin and slice the cucumber to give 'turret' style slices. Place the filled egg halves in the centre of a serving dish and garnish with lettuce quarters and cucumber slices.

Pork and blue cheese bake

Preparation time 20 minutes
Cooking time 30 minutes
Serves 4

IMPERIAL/METRIC	AMERICAN
6 oz./175 g. noodles	⅓ lb. noodles
4 pork chops	4 pork chops
salt and pepper to taste	salt and pepper to taste
1 tablespoon oil	1 tablespoon oil
sauce	**sauce**
1 oz./25 g. butter	2 tablespoons butter
1 oz./25 g. flour	¼ cup all-purpose flour
½ pint/3 dl. milk	1¼ cups milk
3 oz./75 g. blue cheese, crumbled	¾ cup crumbled blue cheese
2 tablespoons chopped green pepper	3 tablespoons chopped green sweet pepper
salt and pepper to taste	salt and pepper to taste

Cook the noodles in boiling, salted water until tender, then rinse and drain. Season the pork chops with salt and pepper. Heat the oil and use to slowly brown the chops on both sides.

Meanwhile prepare the blue cheese sauce. Melt the butter, add the flour and stir until well blended. Cook for 2–3 minutes. Remove from the heat and gradually stir in the milk. Return to heat and bring to the boil, stirring constantly until smooth and thick. Remove from heat, add the crumbled blue cheese and stir until melted. Add the green pepper and season to taste. Mix the sauce with the noodles and pour into an ovenproof casserole. Arrange the pork chops on top of the noodle mixture. Cover and bake in a moderate oven (350°F., 180°C., Gas Mark 4) for 30 minutes.

Parsnip and potato soup

Preparation time 10–15 minutes
Cooking time 50 minutes
Serves 4–6

IMPERIAL/METRIC	AMERICAN
1½ oz./40 g. butter	3 tablespoons butter
1 medium onion, chopped	1 medium onion, chopped
1 large parsnip, chopped	1 large parsnip, chopped
1½ pints/1 litre water	3¾ cups water
2 chicken stock cubes	2 chicken bouillon cubes
1 lb./½ kg. floury potatoes, sliced	1 lb. floury potatoes, sliced
salt and pepper to taste	salt and pepper to taste
good pinch ground allspice	good pinch ground allspice
¼ pint/1½ dl. milk	⅔ cup milk
¼ pint/1½ dl. single cream	⅔ cup coffee cream
to garnish	**to garnish**
chopped chives	chopped chives

Melt the butter in a large saucepan. Use to cook the onion and parsnip over low heat in a covered pan, for 10 minutes. Add the water, stock cubes, potatoes, seasoning and allspice. Bring to the boil, cover and simmer gently for 30 minutes.

Cool slightly and sieve or liquidise. Return to the rinsed-out saucepan, add the milk and reheat. Just before serving in a tureen, pour over the cream in a swirl and sprinkle with chopped chives. If preferred, serve and garnish in individual bowls.

Beef and bacon flan

Preparation time 20 minutes
Cooking time 30 minutes
Serves 4–6

IMPERIAL/METRIC	AMERICAN
8 oz./225 g. self-raising flour	2 cups all-purpose flour sifted with 2 teaspoons baking powder
pinch salt	pinch salt
pinch cayenne pepper	pinch cayenne pepper
4 oz./100 g. butter	½ cup butter
generous ¼ pint/1½ dl. milk	¾ cup milk
topping	**topping**
4 rashers streaky bacon	4 bacon slices
12 oz./350 g. tomatoes	¾ lb. tomatoes
1 oz./25 g. butter	2 tablespoons butter
1 large onion, chopped	1 large onion, chopped
1 (7-oz./200-g.) can corned beef, chopped	1 (7-oz.) can corned beef, chopped
1 tablespoon chopped parsley	1 tablespoon chopped parsley
½ teaspoon sugar	½ teaspoon sugar
salt and pepper to taste	salt and pepper to taste
4 slices processed cheese	4 slices processed cheese

Sieve together the flour, salt and cayenne pepper. Rub in the butter until the mixture resembles fine breadcrumbs and bind with enough milk to form a soft dough. Roll out to an 11-inch (28-cm.) round and place on a floured baking sheet. Roll over ½ inch (1 cm.) of the dough all the way round, to form an edge. Prick the centre lightly with a fork. Brush with milk and bake in a hot oven (425°F., 220°C., Gas Mark 7) for about 20 minutes, until golden.

Meanwhile, to make the topping, remove the rind from the bacon rashers and skin and chop the tomatoes. Melt the butter and use to fry the onion gently until softened. Add the corned beef, mix well and cook gently for 5 minutes. Stir in the tomatoes, parsley, sugar and seasoning and bring to the boil. Cover and simmer for 5 minutes. Spoon the hot tomato mixture on to the scone round and top with bacon rashers in a radial pattern. Place cheese slices in between and return to the oven for a further 10 minutes. Serve with crisp salad and sliced citrus fruit.

Super salmon salad

Preparation time 20 minutes
Serves 4

IMPERIAL/METRIC	AMERICAN
3 large carrots	3 large carrots
1 (7-oz./200-g.) can pink salmon	1 (7-oz.) can pink salmon
1 cucumber	1 cucumber
1 small green sweet pepper	1 small green sweet pepper
2 tablespoons sweetcorn kernels	3 tablespoons corn kernels
4 spring onions, chopped	4 scallions, chopped
4 tablespoons mayonnaise	$\frac{1}{3}$ cup mayonnaise
4 tablespoons soured cream	$\frac{1}{3}$ cup sour cream

Remove thin slices from the carrots with a potato peeler, curl them up and skewer with a pin. Remember to remove the pin before using. Place the curls in cold water until required and grate the remainder of the carrots.

Drain the salmon and flake roughly. Slice the cucumber thinly and deseed the pepper. Cut three neat slices of pepper and reserve, then chop the remaining pepper finely. Mix together lightly the salmon, sweetcorn, grated carrot, spring onion and chopped pepper. Line a serving dish with overlapping cucumber slices and spoon the salmon mixture into the centre. Mix together the mayonnaise and soured cream until smooth, pour over the salmon mixture and garnish with the carrot curls and reserved pepper slices.

Hot baked chicken salad

Preparation time 15 minutes
Cooking time 25 minutes
Serves 4

IMPERIAL/METRIC	AMERICAN
2 oz./50 g. almonds	$\frac{1}{2}$ cup almonds
4 sticks celery, chopped	4 stalks celery, chopped
8 oz./225 g. cooked chicken, diced	1 cup diced cooked chicken
1 teaspoon grated onion	1 teaspoon grated onion
1 teaspoon grated lemon zest	1 teaspoon grated lemon zest
1$\frac{1}{2}$ teaspoons lemon juice	1$\frac{1}{2}$ teaspoons lemon juice
$\frac{1}{2}$ (5-oz./150-g.) can condensed cream of mushroom soup	$\frac{1}{2}$ (5-oz.) can condensed cream of mushroom soup
$\frac{1}{4}$ pint/1$\frac{1}{2}$ dl. mayonnaise or salad cream	$\frac{2}{3}$ cup mayonnaise or salad cream
salt and pepper to taste	salt and pepper to taste
2 oz./50 g. Cheddar cheese, grated	$\frac{1}{2}$ cup grated Cheddar cheese

Roughly chop the almonds and mix together with the celery, chicken, onion, lemon zest and lemon juice. Stir in the soup and the mayonnaise. Season to taste with salt and pepper and divide between four individual ovenproof baking dishes, or pour into an ovenproof casserole. Sprinkle with grated cheese and bake in a moderately hot oven (375°F., 190°C., Gas Mark 5) for 25 minutes, or until thoroughly heated and cheese melted.

Green pasta with garlic sauce

Preparation time 15 minutes
Cooking time 30 minutes
Serves 4

IMPERIAL/METRIC	AMERICAN
8–12 oz./225–350 g. green pasta (tagliatelle verdi)	½–¾ lb. green pasta (tagliatelle verdi)
salt	salt
2 oz./50 g. butter	¼ cup butter
sauce	**sauce**
2 tablespoons olive oil	3 tablespoons olive oil
3 large onions, chopped	3 large onions, chopped
1 tablespoon tomato purée	1 tablespoon tomato paste
2 oz./50 g. grated Parmesan cheese	½ cup grated Parmesan cheese
1 (8-oz./225-g.) can tomatoes	1 (8-oz.) can tomatoes
2 cloves garlic, crushed	2 cloves garlic, crushed
1 bay leaf	1 bay leaf
4 tablespoons red Italian vermouth	⅓ cup red Italian vermouth

Heat the oil and use to fry the onions until softened. Add all the remaining sauce ingredients and stir well. Bring to the boil, cover and simmer for 30 minutes.

Meanwhile, place the pasta into a large saucepan of salted, boiling water and cook gently for about 20 minutes until tender. Drain and toss lightly in the butter. Serve with the garlic sauce.

Delicatessen salad

Preparation time 10 minutes
Cooking time 12 minutes
Serves 4

IMPERIAL/METRIC	AMERICAN
4 thick slices white bread	4 thick slices white bread
4 oz./100 g. tongue, thickly sliced	¼ lb. tongue, thickly sliced
4 oz./100 g. liver sausage, diced	½ cup diced liver sausage
1 (2½-oz./65-g.) can red pimentos, drained	1 (2½-oz.) can red pimientos, drained
4 oz./100 g. long grain rice	generous ½ cup long grain rice
4 tablespoons French dressing	⅓ cup French dressing
¼ teaspoon garlic powder (optional)	¼ teaspoon garlic powder (optional)
1½ oz./40 g. butter	3 tablespoons butter
1 teaspoon oil	1 teaspoon oil
salt and pepper to taste	salt and pepper to taste
few lettuce leaves	few lettuce leaves

Cut the bread, tongue and liver sausage into ½-inch (1-cm.) dice. Cut the pimentos into thin strips and reserve a few for decoration. Cook the rice in boiling salted water until just tender. Drain, pour over fresh hot water and drain again. While still hot, stir in the French dressing (see page 51), tongue, liver sausage, pimento and garlic, if used.

Heat together the butter and oil and use to fry the bread dice until crisp and golden brown. Drain, mix lightly into the rice mixture and season to taste. Chill until required. Spoon the salad mixture into lettuce leaf cups and garnish with the reserved pimento strips.

Tuna bake with cheese swirls

Preparation time 25 minutes
Cooking time 30 minutes
Serves 4–6

IMPERIAL/METRIC	AMERICAN
1 oz./25 g. butter	2 tablespoons butter
1 tablespoon chopped green pepper	1 tablespoon chopped green sweet pepper
1 small onion, chopped	1 small onion, chopped
1 oz./25 g. flour	¼ cup all-purpose flour
½ pint/3 dl. milk	1¼ cups milk
1 (10-oz./275-g.) can condensed cream of celery soup	1 (10-oz.) can condensed cream of celery soup
1 (7-oz./200-g.) can tuna fish, drained	1 (7-oz.) can tuna fish, drained
1 teaspoon lemon juice	1 teaspoon lemon juice
salt and pepper to taste	salt and pepper to taste
cheese swirls	**cheese swirls**
4 oz./100 g. plain flour	1 cup all-purpose flour
1 teaspoon baking powder	1 teaspoon baking powder
¼ teaspoon salt	¼ teaspoon salt
¼ teaspoon cream of tartar	¼ teaspoon cream of tartar
1 teaspoon sugar	1 teaspoon sugar
2 oz./50 g. butter	¼ cup butter
3 fl. oz./about 1 dl. milk	about 6 tablespoons milk
1 oz./25 g. grated Parmesan cheese	¼ cup grated Parmesan cheese

Melt the butter and use to lightly fry the chopped green pepper and chopped onion until soft. Stir in the flour and cook for 2–3 minutes. Remove from the heat and gradually blend in the milk. Return to the heat and bring to the boil, stirring constantly, until thickened. Add the soup, tuna fish and lemon juice. Season to taste with salt and pepper. Pour into an ovenproof casserole.

To make the cheese swirls, sieve the dry ingredients into a bowl and rub in the butter until mixture resembles fine breadcrumbs. Add the milk all at once, stirring lightly. Roll out into a rectangular shape on a lightly floured surface, to ¼-inch (0·5-cm.) thickness. Sprinkle with Parmesan cheese. Roll up, dampen and seal the long edge. Cut into ½-inch (1-cm.) slices. Place the swirls, cut side down, on the tuna mixture and bake in a moderately hot oven (400°F., 200°C., Gas Mark 6) for 30 minutes.

Golden Gate salad

Preparation time 20 minutes
Cooking time about 15 minutes
Serves 4

IMPERIAL/METRIC	AMERICAN
8 oz./¼ kg. new potatoes	½ lb. new potatoes
1 chicken stock cube	1 chicken bouillon cube
½ cucumber	½ cucumber
2 medium carrots	2 medium carrots
8 oz./225 g. Cheddar cheese	½ lb. Cheddar cheese
1 large lettuce	1 large lettuce

Scrub the potatoes and cook until only just tender in boiling, salted water. Drain and chop roughly. Make up the stock cube with only ¼ pint (1½ dl., ⅔ cup) boiling water and pour over the hot chopped potato. Allow to soak in until cold.

Slice the cucumber thinly. Grate the carrots and cheese on a coarse grater. Line a salad bowl with lettuce leaves, arrange the potato salad on this, then the cheese and carrots in alternate heaps around the bowl. Each person may then take a serving of carrot and cheese with some lettuce and potato salad. Use cucumber slices as dividers. Serve with French dressing (see page 51).

Chicken and leek flan

Preparation time 15 minutes
Cooking time 25 minutes
Serves 4

IMPERIAL/METRIC	AMERICAN
1 (8-oz./225-g.) packet frozen shortcrust pastry	1 (8-oz.) package frozen basic pie dough
1 lb./450 g. leeks	1 lb. leeks
1 oz./25 g. butter	2 tablespoons butter
1 oz./25 g. plain flour	¼ cup all-purpose flour
½ pint/3 dl. milk	1¼ cups milk
½ chicken stock cube	½ chicken bouillon cube
salt and pepper to taste	salt and pepper to taste
4 oz./100 g. cooked chicken, chopped	½ cup chopped cooked chicken

Roll out the pastry and use to line a fluted flan ring, placed on a greased baking sheet. Bake blind in a moderately hot oven (375°F., 190°C., Gas Mark 5) for 15 minutes, then remove the paper and baking beans and return to the oven for a further 10 minutes.

To make the filling, cut the leeks into ¼-inch (0·5-cm.) rings and wash well. Melt half the butter and add the leeks. Stir then cover and cook over medium heat for 3 minutes. In a separate pan, melt the remaining butter, stir in the flour and cook gently for a few seconds. Gradually stir in the milk, crumble in the stock cube and cook, stirring constantly, until the sauce is smooth and thick. Adjust the seasoning and stir in the chopped chicken and the leeks. Reheat gently to boiling point, pour into the warm flan case and serve at once.

Spicy pineapple glazed ham

ILLUSTRATED IN COLOUR ON PAGE 7
Preparation time 10 minutes
Cooking time about 2 hours
Serves 8

IMPERIAL/METRIC	AMERICAN
1 (4-lb./1 kg. 800-g.) ham	1 (4-lb.) cured ham
1 onion	1 onion
few peppercorns	few peppercorns
1 bay leaf	1 bay leaf
1 small can pineapple rings	1 small can pineapple rings
2 tablespoons sherry	3 tablespoons sherry
2 tablespoons brown sugar	3 tablespoons brown sugar
cloves	cloves
to decorate	**to decorate**
pineapple rings	pineapple rings
glacé cherries	candied cherries

Put the ham in a saucepan full of cold water and bring to the boil. Add the onion, few peppercorns and bay leaf. Simmer until almost cooked, about 1½ hours. Drain, skin and place the ham in a roasting tin with the pineapple juice. Score the surface into diamond shapes and rub over with a mixture of sherry and brown sugar. Stick a clove in the middle of each diamond and bake in a moderately hot oven (400°F., 200°C., Gas Mark 6), basting frequently with the pineapple juice. Remove from the oven when the skin is shiny and golden brown, and serve hot or cold. Pineapple rings and glacé cherries can be used to decorate the surface.

Note Try soaking the ham in cider before cooking, for extra flavour.

Mexicali eggs

Preparation time 15 minutes
Cooking time 20–25 minutes
Serves 4

IMPERIAL/METRIC	AMERICAN
4 rashers streaky bacon	4 bacon slices
1 tablespoon chopped green pepper	1 tablespoon chopped green sweet pepper
1 tablespoon chopped onion	1 tablespoon chopped onion
1 (8-oz./225-g.) can tomatoes	1 (8-oz.) can tomatoes
½ clove garlic, chopped	½ clove garlic, chopped
4 eggs	4 eggs
salt and pepper to taste	salt and pepper to taste
to garnish	**to garnish**
4 bacon curls	4 bacon curls

Derind and chop the bacon. Place in a frying pan and fry until crisp. Add the green pepper and onion and fry gently until soft. Drain off excess fat and stir in the tomatoes and garlic. Heat through, stirring. Divide the tomato mixture between four ramekin dishes. Carefully slip an egg on top of the tomato mixture in each dish, sprinkle with salt and pepper. Bake in a moderate oven (325°F., 160°C., Gas Mark 3) for 20–25 minutes or until the eggs are set. Garnish with crisp bacon curls and serve with hot buttered toast.

Fish scallops

Preparation time 20 minutes
Cooking time about 25 minutes
Serves 4

IMPERIAL/METRIC	AMERICAN
½ chicken stock cube	½ chicken bouillon cube
½ pint/3 dl. milk	1¼ cups milk
8 oz./225 g. smoked golden fillet	½ lb. smoked golden fillet
8 oz./225 g. white fish fillet	½ lb. white fish fillet
1 oz./25 g. butter	2 tablespoons butter
1 oz./25 g. flour	¼ cup all-purpose flour
1 heaped tablespoon chopped parsley	1 heaped tablespoon chopped parsley
little Parmesan cheese	little Parmesan cheese
1 packet instant potato (serving 4)	1 package instant potato (serving 4)
1 egg	1 egg
good pinch ground nutmeg	good pinch ground nutmeg

Crumble the stock cube into the milk in a saucepan and stir over heat until the cube dissolves. Add the fish to the pan and poach gently for 15 minutes, until tender. Remove the fish with a straining spoon, flake roughly and divide between four deep scallop shells. Strain the liquid from cooking the fish and reserve.

Melt the butter in a saucepan, stir in the flour and cook gently for a minute. Gradually add the fish liquid and bring to the boil, stirring constantly, until the sauce is smooth and thick. Add the parsley, stir well and spoon the sauce over the fish mixture in the shells. Sprinkle with Parmesan cheese and put under a hot grill to brown. Meanwhile, make up the potato and blend in the egg and nutmeg until smooth. Use part to pipe rosettes on the shells and serve the remainder separately.

Danish leek bake

Preparation time 15 minutes
Cooking time about 30 minutes
Serves 4

IMPERIAL/METRIC	AMERICAN
4 medium leeks	4 medium leeks
4 medium potatoes, sliced	4 medium potatoes, sliced
4 oz./100 g. Danish salami, sliced	¼ lb. Danish salami, sliced
1½ oz./40 g. butter	3 tablespoons butter
1½ oz./40 g. flour	6 tablespoons all-purpose flour
½ pint/3 dl. milk	1¼ cups milk
6 oz./175 g. blue cheese, grated	1½ cups grated blue cheese
1 teaspoon Worcestershire sauce	1 teaspoon Worcestershire sauce
salt and pepper to taste	salt and pepper to taste

Remove the outside leaves, roots and most of the green part of the leeks. Insert a knife about 2 inches (5 cm.) from the base end of each leek and pull upwards. Open out and wash the leeks thoroughly under cold, running water. Cook the leeks and potatoes in boiling, salted water until tender. Drain well and reserve ¼ pint (1½ dl., ⅔ cup) of the stock.

Place the potatoes, leeks and salami in an ovenproof dish in layers and keep warm. Meanwhile, melt the butter in a saucepan, stir in the flour and cook for a

minute. Gradually add the milk and reserved stock. Bring to the boil, stirring constantly until the sauce is smooth and thick. Add 4 oz. (125 g., 1 cup) of the cheese and Worcestershire sauce. Stir well and when smooth, taste and adjust seasoning. Pour the sauce over the vegetables and salami in the ovenproof dish. Sprinkle with remaining cheese and place under a hot grill until the cheese is golden and bubbling.
Note If preferred, Cheddar cheese may be used instead of the blue cheese.

Nautilus sandwich

Preparation time 20 minutes
Cooking time 25 minutes
Serves 8

IMPERIAL/METRIC	AMERICAN
4 fl. oz./scant 1½ dl. mayonnaise or salad cream	generous ½ cup mayonnaise or salad cream
1 teaspoon made mustard	1 teaspoon prepared mustard
1 tablespoon chutney	1 tablespoon chutney or relish
4 oz./100 g. ham, minced	½ cup ground cured ham
4 oz./100 g. Cheddar cheese, grated	1 cup grated Cheddar cheese
1 small onion, grated	1 small onion, grated
1 hard-boiled egg, chopped	1 hard-cooked egg, chopped
1 medium French loaf	1 medium French loaf

Mix together lightly the mayonnaise, mustard and chutney then gradually stir in the ham, cheese, onion and egg. Cut the French loaf in half lengthways, but do not cut right through. Take out some of the soft bread centre, to allow more room for the filling. Place the prepared filling in the bread shell, reform into the original shape and wrap closely in foil. Place in a moderate oven (350°F., 180°C., Gas Mark 4) for 25 minutes.

Hot variety loaf

Preparation time 15–20 minutes
Cooking time 1 hour
Serves 4

IMPERIAL/METRIC	AMERICAN
12 oz./350 g. cooked chicken	¾ lb. cooked chicken
4 oz./100 g. chicken livers	¼ lb. chicken livers
1½ oz./40 g. butter	3 tablespoons butter
1½ oz./40 g. browned breadcrumbs	½ cup browned bread crumbs
1 large onion	1 large onion
¼ teaspoon mixed dried herbs	¼ teaspoon mixed dried herbs
½ teaspoon ground nutmeg	½ teaspoon ground nutmeg
2 oz./50 g. fresh white breadcrumbs	1 cup fresh white bread crumbs
1 egg, beaten	1 egg, beaten
¼ pint/1½ dl. strong chicken stock	⅔ cup strong chicken stock
salt and pepper to taste	salt and pepper to taste

Mince together the cooked chicken and raw livers. Grease a 1-lb. (½-kg.) loaf tin with ½ oz. (15 g., 1 tablespoon) of the butter and press two-thirds of the browned breadcrumbs round the bottom and sides of the tin. Finely chop the onion. Melt the remaining butter and use to fry the onion until soft but not coloured. Mix together all the ingredients except the reserved browned breadcrumbs and press into the prepared tin. Cover with foil and bake in a moderate oven (350°F., 180°C., Gas Mark 4) for 1 hour. Turn the loaf out of the tin and sprinkle with remaining breadcrumbs. Serve with cooked cut green beans.

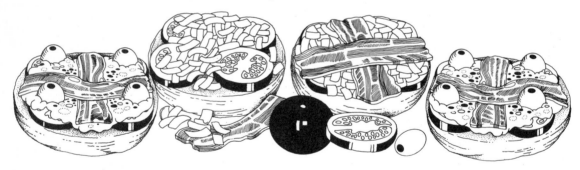

Quick Spanish pizzas

Preparation time 10 minutes
Cooking time about 8 minutes
Serves 4

IMPERIAL/METRIC	AMERICAN
4 baps	4 hamburger rolls
4 medium tomatoes	4 medium tomatoes
4 oz./100 g. Cheddar cheese, grated	1 cup grated Cheddar cheese
salt, pepper and paprika pepper to taste	salt, pepper and paprika pepper to taste
8 thin rashers streaky bacon, halved	8 thin bacon slices, halved
16 stuffed green olives	16 stuffed green olives

Cut the baps in half and toast lightly on each side. Cut each tomato into 4 slices and place on cut side of the baps. Sprinkle with cheese and season with salt, pepper and lastly paprika. Place 2 pieces of bacon diagonally across each bap and place under a hot grill until the bacon is crisp and cheese is melted and bubbling. Garnish each bap with 4 olive halves before serving.

Devilled ham pudding

Preparation time 10–15 minutes
Cooking time 35–45 minutes
Serves 4

IMPERIAL/METRIC	AMERICAN
1½ oz./40 g. butter, softened	3 tablespoons softened butter
1 tablespoon made mustard	1 tablespoon prepared mustard
1 tablespoon fruit chutney	1 tablespoon fruit relish
6 thin slices white bread	6 thin slices white bread
3 tomatoes	3 tomatoes
3 thick slices cooked ham	3 thick slices cooked cured ham
1 tablespoon melted butter	1 tablespoon melted butter
3 eggs	3 eggs
salt and pepper to taste	salt and pepper to taste
1 pint/6 dl. milk	2½ cups milk

Mix together the butter, mustard and chutney. Remove crusts from the bread and spread with the mixture. Slice the tomatoes thinly and reserve three slices for the garnish. Place the ham on three slices of bread, top with tomato slices and cover with remaining bread slices. Cut each sandwich into 4 triangles and place overlapping in a shallow, buttered ovenproof dish. Brush the top layers of bread with melted butter. Beat together the eggs, seasoning and milk and strain over the bread dish. Garnish with reserved, halved tomato slices and bake in a moderate oven (350°F., 180°C., Gas Mark 4) for 35–45 minutes, or until the 'custard' is set.

Smothered sausages

Preparation time 10 minutes
Cooking time about 30 minutes
Serves 4

IMPERIAL/METRIC	AMERICAN
4 oz./100 g. onion	1 cup chopped onion
1 (8-oz./225 g.) can hot dogs	1 (8-oz.) can frankfurters or hot dogs
salt and pepper to taste	salt and pepper to taste
12 oz./350 g. mashed potato	1½ cups mashed potato
little milk	little milk
1 egg, beaten	1 egg, beaten

Finely chop the onion and mix with 2 tablespoons liquid from the can of hot dogs. Place this mixture in a greased ovenproof dish and put into a moderately hot oven (375°F., 190°C., Gas Mark 5) for 5 minutes. Place the drained sausages in the dish and season with salt and pepper. Beat the potato until smooth with a little milk and seasoning to taste. (If preferred, use a large packet of instant potato.) Pipe or fork the potato over the sausages and brush with beaten egg. Place in the oven at the same temperature as above for a further 25–30 minutes.

Croquettes de Camembert

Preparation time 10–15 minutes plus cooling time
Cooking time 2 minutes per croquette
Serves 4

IMPERIAL/METRIC	AMERICAN
2 oz./50 g. flour	½ cup all-purpose flour
¼ pint/1½ dl. milk	⅔ cup milk
8 oz./225 g. Camembert cheese	½ lb. Camembert cheese
2½ oz./65 g. butter	5 tablespoons butter
pinch cayenne pepper	pinch cayenne pepper
pinch ground nutmeg	pinch ground nutmeg
2 eggs	2 eggs
salt and black pepper to taste	salt and black pepper to taste
2 teaspoons oil	2 teaspoons oil
oil for frying	oil for frying

Blend together the flour and milk. Remove the rind from the Camembert and add to flour mixture with the butter, cayenne and nutmeg. Bring to the boil and simmer over a low heat, stirring continuously, for about 3 minutes. Allow to cool and spread the mixture on a tray. Mould into small even-sized flat rounds.

Whisk the eggs until stiff, add seasoning and oil. Dip each croquette into this mixture, then fry quickly in hot oil for 2 minutes. Serve with very thin fingers of toast and a tossed green salad.

Savoury pancakes

Preparation time 20 minutes
Cooking time 15–20 minutes
Serves 4

IMPERIAL/METRIC	AMERICAN
4 oz./100 g. plain flour	1 cup all-purpose flour
pinch salt	pinch salt
1 egg	1 egg
½ pint/3 dl. milk	1¼ cups milk
1 tablespoon oil	1 tablespoon oil
oil for frying	oil for frying
filling	**filling**
1½ oz./40 g. butter	3 tablespoons butter
1½ oz./40 g. flour	6 tablespoons all-purpose flour
¾ pint/4 dl. milk	2 cups milk
6 oz./175 g. luncheon meat, diced	¾ cup diced luncheon meat
6 oz./175 g. Edam cheese, diced	1 cup diced Dutch cheese
salt and pepper to taste	salt and pepper to taste
to garnish	**to garnish**
1 tomato, sliced	1 tomato, sliced
parsley sprigs	parsley sprigs

Sieve the flour and salt into a basin. Add the egg to the dry ingredients then gradually add the milk, beating well, until the batter is smooth. Beat in the oil.

Heat a little oil in a small frying pan and use to fry thin pancakes until golden brown on both sides – use about 2 tablespoons batter for each pancake.

For the filling, melt the butter in a saucepan, add the flour and cook for a minute. Remove from the heat and stir in the milk. Return to the heat and bring to the boil, stirring. Add the luncheon meat and cheese, season well and reheat gently until the cheese begins to melt. Spoon some of this filling into the centre of each pancake and roll up. Garnish with tomato slices and parsley.

Orange summer soufflé

ILLUSTRATED IN COLOUR ON PAGE 7
Preparation time 15–20 minutes plus setting time
Serves 4

IMPERIAL/METRIC	AMERICAN
3 eggs, separated	3 eggs, separated
2 oz./50 g. castor sugar	$\frac{1}{4}$ cup sugar
grated rind and juice of 1 orange	grated rind and juice of 1 orange
$\frac{1}{4}$ oz./7 g. gelatine	1 envelope gelatin
3 tablespoons cold water	4 tablespoons cold water
$\frac{1}{4}$ pint/1$\frac{1}{2}$ dl. double cream	$\frac{2}{3}$ cup heavy cream
1 tablespoon Grand Marnier	1 tablespoon Grand Marnier
to decorate	**to decorate**
whipped cream	whipped cream
1 orange, sliced	1 orange, sliced

Beat the egg yolks, sugar, rind and juice in a basin over hot water, until thick and creamy. Dissolve the gelatine in the water over a low heat. Stir carefully into the yolk mixture. When on the point of setting, fold in the lightly whipped cream, whisked egg whites and Grand Marnier. Pour into a 5–6-inch (12–15-cm.) soufflé dish, which has a band of greaseproof paper tied round it, to come 2 inches (5 cm.) higher than the dish. Leave in a cool place until set. Remove the paper carefully and decorate with piped cream and slices of orange.

Mandarin liqueur creams

Preparation time 15 minutes plus cooling time
Serves 4

IMPERIAL/METRIC	AMERICAN
1 oz./25 g. seedless raisins	3 tablespoons seedless raisins
2 tablespoons Cointreau	3 tablespoons Cointreau
1 small can evaporated milk, chilled	1 small can evaporated milk, chilled
1 orange jelly	1 package orange-flavored gelatin
1 (8-oz./225-g.) can mandarin oranges	1 (8-oz.) can mandarin oranges
to decorate	**to decorate**
$\frac{1}{4}$ pint/1$\frac{1}{2}$ dl. whipped cream	$\frac{2}{3}$ cup whipped cream
1 tablespoon toasted almonds	1 tablespoon toasted almonds

Soak the raisins in the liqueur until plump. Whisk the evaporated milk until thick. Dissolve the jelly in $\frac{1}{4}$ pint (1$\frac{1}{2}$ dl., $\frac{2}{3}$ cup) hot water, add the syrup from the can and allow to cool. When the jelly is on the point of setting, whisk it into the thick evaporated milk.

Half fill four small glass dishes with mandarin segments, reserving a few for decoration, and top with the plumped raisins. Add the soaking liquid to the jelly mixture and divide this between the dishes. To serve, arrange the remaining mandarin segments on top and pipe rosettes of cream. Scatter with almonds.

Hearty main
courses for lunch or dinner

Sunday lunch is a popular choice for family entertaining and, now and again, a simple main meal has to be 'stretched' to include a guest. This is not the sort of occasion when cost is unimportant, as it might be for a formal planned dinner party. Fortunately, there are lots of appetising but reasonable alternatives, each with a touch of style to make it special enough to pay compliment to the guests. Even Beefy crumble is more fun than simple minced beef. As for a joint, pork seems to be the least expensive choice, a stuffed pork joint goes a very long way.

Glance through these recipes and choose a main dish. A starter is not needed, but if the sweet doesn't seem to be adequate for extra portions, follow up with a cheese board, choice of sliced bread, crispbreads and biscuits, butter and a side dish of celery curls, radishes or sliced apple – all good partners with cheese.

The easiest sweet of all is a brick of ice cream or a few scoops from a litre container from the freezer. Sweet sauces are easy to contrive and hot ones are the most dramatic. Try out spiced fruit sauce, using syrup from canned fruit thickened with arrowroot, spiced with cinnamon, ginger or nutmeg, and some chopped fruit stirred in at the end.

Another way to zip up the main dishes is to serve a second vegetable, rather than more cabbage or Brussels sprouts. Carrots can be frozen, canned or fresh. Fresh carrots cook quickly if quartered lengthways, moistened with the juice and grated zest of an orange, with a knob of butter (and a little more water added) then cooked, covered, until all the liquid is absorbed. Season last of all carefully with salt, pepper and grated nutmeg.

Tuna pilchard plait (page 27) with piquant tomato sauce (page 26), steak, kidney and mushroom pie (page 22) and savoury mince parcels (page 35).

Potatoes, good enough to grace any table, can be made with instant mix, though I prefer to choose one with added vitamin C. Made with half milk, half water, an egg whipped in with some butter, they need only the finishing touch of salt, pepper and some spice, although nutmeg is generally accepted as best. For good measure, stir in grated hard cheese, or crumbled if it won't grate, while the potato is very hot so that it melts slightly. Baked jacket potatoes get a festive air from being cut with a cross on top, squeezed up slightly and filled to brimming with seasoned sour cream and chives or garlic butter.

Sometimes the service of the dish makes it fit for guests. Always have a large ovenproof dish, deep enough to hold enough cooked pasta (green ribbon noodles look good) or saffron rice to display portions of meat, fish or chicken attractively. Baked frozen chicken joints coated in spiced batter, turn out crisp and golden from the oven. Pile them up, letting a border of rice or noodles show through, and top with a little rich tomato sauce, serving the rest in a sauceboat. Fish portions, baked in the oven in milk, look good on white rice and should just be masked in freshly made mushroom sauce. A quick tip is to use concentrated cream of mushroom soup, diluted only with half as much strained milk from poaching the fish. Even a few ounces of freshly fried mushrooms, cooked in butter, make a delicious garnish. Split almonds, tossed in butter and sprinkled with salt, are more unusual still. Pork chops, grilled or baked, are super on noodles; use their juices, mixed with apple chutney, as a sauce. As you can now see, it is truly not difficult to turn a hearty family meal into a feast with a few added touches.

21

Steak, kidney and mushroom pie

ILLUSTRATED IN COLOUR ON PAGE 20
Preparation time 25 minutes
Cooking time 2½–3 hours in total
Serves 4-5

IMPERIAL/METRIC	AMERICAN
1½ lb./700 g. stewing steak	1½ lb. beef stew meat
8 oz./225 g. kidney	½ lb. kidney
1 oz./25 g. plain flour	¼ cup all-purpose flour
salt and pepper to taste	salt and pepper to taste
1 oz./25 g. lard	2 tablespoons oil or lard
1 medium onion, chopped	1 medium onion, chopped
4 oz./100 g. button mushrooms	1 cup button mushrooms
½ pint/3 dl. beef stock	1¼ cups beef stock
8 oz./225 g. flaky pastry mix	½ lb. puff paste mix
1 egg, beaten	1 egg, beaten

Cut the steak into 1-inch (2·5-cm.) cubes and the kidney into ½-inch (1-cm.) cubes. Put the flour and plenty of seasoning in a polythene bag. Add the steak and kidney and shake the bag until all the meat is coated with flour. Reserve any flour in the bag and remove the meat. Melt the lard and use to fry the onion until just tender but not brown. Add the meat and brown quickly on all sides. Add the mushrooms and cook for a minute. Stir in the reserved flour, if any, then add the stock and bring to the boil, stirring constantly. Cover and simmer gently for 1½–2 hours, or until the meat is tender. Leave until cold.

Put the meat and mushrooms into a pie dish with enough gravy to come halfway up the dish. Place a pie funnel in the centre to support the pastry top. Prepare the flaky pastry mix according to the instructions, then roll out to about 1 inch (2·5 cm.) larger than the top of the pie dish. Cut out a long strip of pastry about ½ inch (1 cm.) wide to fit the rim of the dish, and a pastry lid. Moisten the rim of the dish and press on the pastry strip. Moisten this strip and place the lid on. Press down well to seal the edges and trim off excess pastry. Knock up the edges together and flute with a knife. Re-roll the pastry trimmings and cut out leaves to decorate the pie. Dampen them and arrange in place. Brush with beaten egg and bake in a hot oven (425°F., 220°C., Gas Mark 7) for 20 minutes. Reduce the oven heat to moderate (350°F., 180°C., Gas Mark 4) for a further 20–30 minutes, or until the pastry is well risen and golden brown, and filling is tender.

Cottage cheese and noodle kugel

Preparation time 20 minutes
Cooking time about 45 minutes
Serves 4

IMPERIAL/METRIC	AMERICAN
4 oz./100 g. short-cut noodles	1 cup short-cut noodles
2 oz./50 g. butter	¼ cup butter
¼ pint/1½ dl. soured cream	⅔ cup sour cream
8 oz./225 g. cottage cheese with chives	1 cup cottage cheese with chives
1 tablespoon Parmesan cheese	1 tablespoon Parmesan cheese
salt and black pepper to taste	salt and black pepper to taste
2 eggs, beaten	2 eggs, beaten
to garnish	**to garnish**
watercress	watercress

Cook the noodles in 2 pints (generous litre, 5 cups) well salted, boiling water for about 10 minutes until just tender. Drain well. Melt the butter in the same pan and mix in the cooked noodles. Blend together the soured cream, cottage cheese and Parmesan in a large bowl and mix in the buttered noodles. Season well with salt and black pepper and bind with the beaten eggs. Oil a 1-pint (½-litre, 2½-cup) ring mould and pack in the noodle mixture. Cover with grease-proof paper and bake in a moderately hot oven (375°F., 190°C., Gas Mark 5) for 45 minutes or until set. Unmould on to a warm serving dish and fill the ring with chopped hard-boiled eggs in fresh tomato sauce, if liked. Serve garnished with sprigs of water-cress.

Note This recipe solves the problem of how to serve a hearty main dish to a vegetarian guest.

Dappled chicken

Preparation time 20 minutes
Cooking time about 40 minutes
Serves 4

IMPERIAL/METRIC	AMERICAN
1 chicken stock cube	1 chicken bouillon cube
12 oz./350 g. chicken breast, diced	¾ lb. chicken breast, diced
1 large onion, sliced	1 large onion, sliced
4 sticks celery, chopped	4 stalks celery, chopped
¼ pint/1½ dl. milk	⅔ cup milk
2 red-skinned eating apples	2 red-skinned eating apples
2 oz./50 g. butter	¼ cup butter
1 oz./25 g. flour	¼ cup all-purpose flour
salt and pepper to taste	salt and pepper to taste
1 packet instant potato	1 package instant potato

Make up the chicken stock cube with ¾ pint (4½ dl., 2 cups) boiling water and use to poach the chicken until tender. Drain and use the stock again to cook the onion and celery until soft. Drain and reserve ¼ pint (1½ dl., ⅔ cup) of the cooking stock. Make this up to ½ pint (3 dl., 1¼ cups) with the milk.

Peel, core and chop one apple. Place the chicken, onion, celery, and chopped apple in the base of an ovenproof dish. Melt half the butter in a saucepan, stir in the flour and cook for 2 minutes. Gradually add the flavoured milk and bring to the boil, stirring constantly, until the sauce is smooth and thickened. Taste and correct seasoning. Pour the sauce over the chicken mixture.

Make up the potato and beat in the remaining butter to give a smooth creamy texture. Pipe potato around the edge of the dish. Place under a hot grill for 5 minutes to brown the potato. Core and slice the remaining apple and arrange on top as the garnish.

Beefy crumble

Preparation time 20 minutes
Cooking time 40–45 minutes
Serves 4

IMPERIAL/METRIC	AMERICAN
2 rashers fat streaky bacon	2 bacon slices
1 small onion, grated	1 small onion, grated
12 oz./350 g. minced beef	1½ cups ground beef
1 beef stock cube	1 beef bouillon cube
4 oz./100 g. plain flour	1 cup all-purpose flour
2 oz./50 g. butter	¼ cup butter
1 teaspoon salt	1 teaspoon salt
¼ teaspoon pepper	¼ teaspoon pepper
2 oz./50 g. cheese, grated	½ cup grated cheese

Derind or cut the bacon into strips, render out the fat in a frying pan until the bacon is crisp. Remove and keep warm. Fry the onion and beef in the same pan until lightly browned – takes 5–10 minutes, add the bacon and the stock cube, dissolved in ½ pint (3 dl., 1¼ cups) boiling water. Sprinkle in 1 tablespoon of the flour, stir well and transfer to a baking dish.

Rub the butter into the remaining flour, sieved with salt and pepper, until the mixture resembles fine breadcrumbs. Sprinkle over the meat mixture, pressing down well, and top with grated cheese. Bake in the centre of a moderately hot oven (375°F., 190°C., Gas Mark 5) for 40–45 minutes.

Liver hot pot

Preparation time 20 minutes
Cooking time 1 hour 30 minutes
Serves 4

IMPERIAL/METRIC	AMERICAN
1 large cooking apple	1 large baking apple
2½ oz./65 g. butter	5 tablespoons butter
12 oz./350 g. pig's liver, sliced	¾ lb. pork liver, sliced
4 oz./100 g. bacon, diced	½ cup diced bacon or cured ham
8 oz./¼ kg. onions, chopped	2 cups chopped onion
2 carrots, sliced	2 carrots, sliced
salt and pepper to taste	salt and pepper to taste
½ pint/3 dl. water or stock	1¼ cups water or stock
2 teaspoons gravy powder	2 teaspoons gravy powder
1 lb./½ kg. potatoes, sliced	1 lb. potatoes, sliced
to garnish	**to garnish**
sprig of parsley	sprig of parsley

Peel, core and chop the apple. Melt 2 oz. (50 g., ¼ cup) of the butter and use to fry the liver and bacon until lightly browned. Remove the liver and bacon. Add the onion and carrots to the fat remaining in the pan and fry until the onion is just beginning to soften.

Arrange the liver and bacon in a greased ovenproof casserole in alternate layers with the onion, carrot, apple and seasoning. Add the water or stock to the frying pan. Moisten the gravy powder with 2 tablespoons water. Stir it into the frying pan and bring to the boil, stirring constantly, until thickened. Pour over the casserole. Melt the remaining butter and use to brush the potato slices, which have been overlapped on top of the casserole. Cover with a lid or foil and cook in a moderate oven (325°F., 160°C., Gas Mark 3) for about 1 hour. Remove the lid or foil, raise the oven temperature to moderately hot (400°F., 200°C., Gas Mark 6) and cook for a further 30 minutes. Garnish with parsley.

Note If preferred, fry the potato slices separately on both sides in very little fat until golden brown. Arrange overlapping on top of the casserole for the last 20 minutes cooking time.

Cod creole

Preparation time 15 minutes
Cooking time about 20 minutes
Serves 4

IMPERIAL/METRIC	AMERICAN
1 onion	1 onion
1 green pepper	1 green sweet pepper
1 oz./25 g. butter	2 tablespoons butter
1 tablespoon flour	1 tablespoon flour
12 oz./350 g. canned tomatoes	1½ cups canned tomatoes
4 tablespoons tomato purée	⅓ cup tomato paste
¼ pint/1½ dl. chicken stock	⅔ cup chicken stock
dash Tabasco sauce	dash Tabasco sauce
pinch sugar	pinch sugar
salt and pepper to taste	salt and pepper to taste
bouquet garni	bouquet garni
1 lb./½ kg. cod	1 lb. cod or similar fish
grated lemon zest	grated lemon zest

Chop the onion finely and deseed and chop the green pepper. Melt the butter and use to sauté these until softened. Stir in the flour until smooth and then add the tomatoes, tomato purée, stock, Tabasco sauce, sugar, salt and bouquet garni. Cut the cod into wedges and add to the pan. Bring to the boil, cover and simmer for 15 minutes. Adjust seasoning and serve garnished with grated lemon zest. Serve with fluffy boiled rice.

Apple stuffed mackerel

Preparation time 15 minutes plus time to prepare garnish
Cooking time about 40 minutes
Serves 4

IMPERIAL/METRIC	AMERICAN
4 medium mackerel, cleaned	4 medium mackerel or similar fish, cleaned
stuffing	**stuffing**
1 large cooking apple	1 large baking apple
3 oz./75 g. butter	6 tablespoons butter
1 medium onion, chopped	1 medium onion, chopped
4 oz./100 g. white bread, cubed	2 cups diced white bread
1 tablespoon chopped parsley	1 tablespoon chopped parsley
½ teaspoon dried basil	½ teaspoon dried basil
grated zest of 1 lemon	grated zest of 1 lemon
salt and pepper to taste	salt and pepper to taste
to garnish	**to garnish**
2 cooking apples	2 baking apples
4 oz./100 g. butter	½ cup butter
parsley sprigs	parsley sprigs

Remove heads from the mackerel. Peel, core and chop the apple. Melt the butter and use to fry the onion until softened, then add the bread cubes. Mix in the chopped apple and continue cooking until it is soft. Add the herbs and lemon zest and season well. Stuff the mackerel and secure closed with small skewers or wooden cocktail sticks. Place in a greased ovenproof dish and bake in a moderate oven (350°F., 180°C., Gas Mark 4) for about 40 minutes, or until golden brown and cooked through.

To prepare the garnish, core the unpeeled apples and slice thickly. Melt the butter and use to fry the apple slices until golden brown on each side, turning once. Arrange overlapping fried apple slices along each side of the mackerel and garnish with fresh sprigs of parsley.

French rabbit casserole

Preparation time 10–15 minutes
Cooking time 1 hour
Serves 4–6

IMPERIAL/METRIC	AMERICAN
2 tablespoons oil	3 tablespoons oil
2 onions, sliced	2 onions, sliced
1 green pepper	1 green sweet pepper
12 oz./350 g. courgettes	¾ lb. small zucchini
4 oz./100 g. mushrooms, chopped	1 cup chopped mushrooms
1¼ lb./600 g. boned rabbit, diced	1¼ lb. boned rabbit, diced
1 tablespoon tomato purée	1 tablespoon tomato paste
½ chicken stock cube dissolved in ½ pint (3 dl.) water	½ chicken bouillon cube dissolved in 1¼ cups water
garlic salt (optional)	garlic salt (optional)
salt and pepper to taste	salt and pepper to taste

Heat the oil in a large saucepan and use to fry the onions gently for 5 minutes, until soft but not coloured. Deseed and chop the pepper and slice the courgettes. Add these to the saucepan with the mushrooms and diced rabbit. Mix together the tomato purée and stock and add this mixture to the saucepan. Stir well and add seasoning to taste. Bring to the boil, cover and simmer gently for 1 hour. This dish can also be cooked slowly in the oven. Serve with floury boiled potatoes.

Pollo Espagnola

Preparation time 10–15 minutes
Cooking time about 1 hour 30 minutes
Serves 4

IMPERIAL/METRIC	AMERICAN
4 chicken portions, skinned	4 chicken pieces, skinned
1 oz./25 g. seasoned cornflour	¼ cup seasoned cornstarch
2 tablespoons corn oil	3 tablespoons corn oil
1 onion, finely chopped	1 onion, finely chopped
2 carrots, sliced	2 carrots, sliced
1 (5¼-oz./150-g.) can tomato purée	1 (5¼-oz.) can tomato paste
2 chicken stock cubes	2 chicken bouillon cubes
1¼ pints/¾ litre water	3 cups water
¼ pint/1½ dl. sherry	⅔ cup sherry
4 oz./100 g. mushrooms, sliced	1 cup sliced mushrooms
to garnish	**to garnish**
chopped parsley	chopped parsley

Coat the chicken portions in seasoned cornflour. Heat the corn oil and use to brown the chicken portions on all sides. Remove the portions to an ovenproof casserole. Finely chop the onion and sauté with the carrots in the remaining corn oil until golden. Stir in the tomato purée, stock cubes, water and sherry and bring to the boil, stirring constantly.

Pour the sauce into the casserole. Cover and cook in a moderate oven (325°F., 160°C., Gas Mark 3) for 1 hour. Add the mushrooms and cook for a further 15 minutes. Sprinkle with chopped parsley before serving.

Lamb and butter bean casserole

Preparation time 10 minutes
Cooking time about 3 hours
Serves 4

IMPERIAL/METRIC	AMERICAN
2 lb./1 kg. boned shoulder of lamb, diced	2 lb. boned shoulder of lamb, diced
2 tablespoons corn oil	3 tablespoons corn oil
6 small onions	6 small onions
1 beef stock cube	1 beef bouillon cube
¾ pint/4 dl. boiling water	2 cups boiling water
1 (15-oz./425-g.) can tomatoes	1 (15-oz.) can tomatoes
1 (15-oz./425-g.) can butter beans, drained	1 (15-oz.) can butter, navy or kidney beans

Trim off any excess fat from the meat. Heat the oil in a flameproof casserole and use to fry the onions until just golden. Add the meat and fry until browned on all sides. Dissolve the stock cube in the boiling water and add to the casserole with the tomatoes. Stir well, bring to the boil, cover and simmer very gently for 2½ hours. Add the butter beans and cook for a further 15–20 minutes, until the meat is tender.

Piquant tomato sauce

Preparation time 10 minutes
Cooking time about 20 minutes
Serves 4–6

IMPERIAL/METRIC	AMERICAN
1 small green pepper	1 small green sweet pepper
½ oz./15 g. butter	1 tablespoon butter
1 small onion	1 small onion
1 (15½-oz./440-g.) can peeled tomatoes, sieved	1 (15½-oz.) can peeled tomatoes, sieved
juice of ½ lemon	juice of ½ lemon
1 tablespoon Worcestershire sauce	1 tablespoon Worcestershire sauce
salt and pepper to taste	salt and pepper to taste

Deseed and chop the green pepper. Melt the butter and use to fry the chopped onion and green pepper until just tender. Stir in the sieved tomatoes, lemon juice, Worcestershire sauce and seasoning. Bring to the boil and simmer gently, uncovered, for 10–15 minutes, until the sauce has thickened.

Tuna pilchard plait

ILLUSTRATED IN COLOUR ON PAGE 20
Preparation time 20–25 minutes
Cooking time 20–25 minutes
Serves 4

IMPERIAL/METRIC	AMERICAN
1 (1-lb./450-g.) can pilchards in tomato sauce	1 (1-lb.) can pilchards in tomato sauce
1 (7½-oz./210-g.) can tuna	1 (7½-oz.) can tuna
1 small onion	1 small onion
2 oz./50 g. mushrooms	½ cup mushrooms
½ oz./15 g. lard	1 tablespoon lard
1 teaspoon plain flour	1 teaspoon flour
2 tablespoons chopped parsley	3 tablespoons chopped parsley
2 tablespoons tomato ketchup	3 tablespoons tomato catsup
salt and pepper to taste	salt and pepper to taste
12 oz./350 g. shortcrust pastry mix	12 oz. pie crust mix
about 6 tablespoons milk	about 7 tablespoons milk
beaten egg to glaze	beaten egg to glaze

Remove any large bones from the pilchards and tuna, then flake the fish. Finely chop the onion and mushrooms. Melt the lard in a saucepan and use to fry the onion and mushroom until softened. Stir in the flour and cook for a minute. Remove from the heat and stir in parsley, ketchup, fish and seasoning. Mix well.

Put the pastry mix into a bowl and add enough milk (4–6 tablespoons) to make a stiff dough. Roll out the pastry on a floured board and trim to a 12-inch (31-cm.) square. Place the pilchard and tuna mixture down the centre third of the pastry, leaving ½ inch (1 cm.) clear at the top and bottom. Make cuts at an angle, from the edges of pastry to within ½ inch (1 cm.) of the filling, at 1-inch (2·5-cm.) intervals on both sides. Brush the edges of the pastry with water. Fold in the ½-inch (1-cm.) of pastry at the top and bottom, then fold alternate strips of pastry from the sides over the filling to form a plait and enclose the filling completely. Brush with egg. Place on a greased baking sheet and bake at 400°F., 200°C., Gas Mark 6 for 20–25 minutes until golden brown. Serve hot or cold with Piquant tomato sauce.

Pork roly-poly

Preparation time 20 minutes
Cooking time about 3 hours
Serves 4

IMPERIAL/METRIC	AMERICAN
1 tablespoon oil	1 tablespoon oil
1 small onion, chopped	1 small onion, chopped
8 oz./225 g. bladebone of pork, minced	1 cup ground picnic shoulder of pork
8 oz./225 g. minced beef	1 cup ground beef
2 tablespoons tomato ketchup	3 tablespoons tomato catsup
pinch dried basil	pinch dried basil
salt and pepper to taste	salt and pepper to taste
pastry	**pastry**
8 oz./225 g. self-raising flour	2 cups all-purpose flour sifted with 2 teaspoons baking powder
pinch salt	
4 oz./100 g. shredded suet	scant 1 cup chopped beef suet
¼ pint/1½ dl. water	⅔ cup water

Heat the oil and use to fry the onion gently until soft but not coloured. Add the pork and beef and stir over high heat until the meat changes colour. Cover and cook very gently for 10 minutes. Drain off excess liquid and stir in the ketchup and basil. Season to taste with salt and pepper.

Sieve the flour and salt into a basin and mix in the suet. Add sufficient cold water to make a soft dough and roll out to an oblong. Spread the filling mixture on the pastry to within ½ inch (1 cm.) of the edges. Damp the edges, roll up like a Swiss roll and tuck the ends underneath. Wrap the roll in greased greaseproof paper and then in foil and steam for 2½ hours. Serve hot with cooked mixed vegetables.

Savoury turkey drumsticks

Preparation time 15 minutes
Cooking time about 1 hour
Serves 4

IMPERIAL/METRIC	AMERICAN
3 tablespoons cooking oil	¼ cup cooking oil
4 turkey drumsticks	4 turkey drumsticks
1 small green pepper	1 small green sweet pepper
8 very small onions, peeled	8 tiny onions, peeled
4 rashers streaky bacon, chopped	4 bacon slices, chopped
1½ oz./40 g. flour	6 tablespoons all-purpose flour
¾ pint/4 dl. chicken stock or water	2 cups chicken stock or water
1 teaspoon Tabasco sauce	1 teaspoon Tabasco sauce
salt	salt
4 oz./100 g. button mushrooms	1 cup button mushrooms
4–6 oz./100–175 g. long grain rice	scant 1 cup long grain rice

Heat the oil in a frying pan and use to fry the turkey drumsticks quickly to brown on all sides. Remove the turkey to an ovenproof casserole. Deseed and slice the green pepper. Add the onions, green pepper and bacon to the frying pan and fry for 4 minutes. Drain and transfer to the casserole. Stir the flour into the remaining oil in the pan, cook for 2 minutes, stirring constantly. Gradually add the stock or water and bring to the boil, stirring constantly. Add the Tabasco and salt to taste. Pour the sauce into the casserole and stir in the mushrooms. Cover and cook in a moderate oven (350°F., 180°C., Gas Mark 4) for about 1 hour, until the turkey is tender. Meanwhile cook the rice in boiling, salted water until tender. Drain and stir a few spoonfuls into the casserole just before serving. Serve with the remainder of the cooked rice.

Orchard chicken

Preparation time 15–20 minutes
Cooking time about 45 minutes
Serves 6

IMPERIAL/METRIC	AMERICAN
6 chicken quarters	6 chicken pieces
1 bay leaf	1 bay leaf
1 large sprig parsley	1 large sprig parsley
salt and pepper to taste	salt and pepper to taste
2 tablespoons oil	3 tablespoons oil
1 oz./25 g. plain flour	¼ cup all-purpose flour
2 onions, chopped	2 onions, chopped
1 teaspoon crushed coriander seeds	1 teaspoon crushed coriander seeds
¼ teaspoon ground cinnamon	¼ teaspoon ground cinnamon
¼ teaspoon powdered saffron	¼ teaspoon powdered saffron
3 pieces stem ginger	3 pieces stem ginger
1 lb./½ kg. Conference pears	1 lb. eating pears
8 oz./¼ kg. eating apples	½ lb. eating apples
8 oz./¼ kg. plums or apricots	½ lb. plums or apricots
1 tablespoon ginger syrup	1 tablespoon ginger syrup
lemon juice to taste	lemon juice to taste
1 tablespoon chopped fresh parsley	1 tablespoon chopped fresh parsley

Skin the chicken joints. Divide the legs into the drumstick and thigh and then remove the bone. Remove the wing pinions and backbone from the breast portions. Put these bones into a saucepan with the bay leaf, parsley sprig, salt and pepper. Cover with water and simmer to make stock.

Heat the oil in a flameproof casserole, coat the chicken portions with flour and fry in the hot oil until crisp and golden all over. Remove from the pan, add the onion to the remaining oil and fry gently until just turning colour. Replace the chicken and add sufficient stock to cover the joints. Mix in the coriander, cinnamon, saffron and chopped ginger. Bring to the boil, cover and simmer for 20 minutes. Peel, slice and core the pears and apples. Halve and stone the plums or apricots. Add the fruit and ginger syrup to the casserole. Cover and simmer gently for a further 10 minutes, until the chicken is tender. Sharpen to taste with lemon juice. Serve sprinkled with chopped parsley.

Somerset sausage pie

Preparation time 15–20 minutes
Cooking time 50 minutes
Serves 4

IMPERIAL/METRIC	AMERICAN
8 oz./225 g. streaky bacon	½ lb. bacon slices
8 oz./225 g. pork sausagemeat	½ lb. pork sausagemeat
8 oz./225 g. onions, chopped	2 cups chopped onion
1 small swede, chopped	1 small swede or rutabaga, chopped
salt and pepper to taste	salt and pepper to taste
¼ pint/1½ dl. cider	⅔ cup cider
pastry	**pastry**
8 oz./225 g. plain flour	2 cups all-purpose flour
pinch salt	pinch salt
4 oz./100 g. butter	½ cup butter
2 tablespoons water	3 tablespoons water
1 egg, beaten	1 egg, beaten

Derind the bacon and dice neatly. Mix together the bacon, sausagemeat, onion, swede and seasoning and place this mixture in a 2-pint (1-litre, 5-cup) pie dish. Pour over the cider.

Sieve the flour and salt into a bowl and rub in the butter until the mixture resembles fine breadcrumbs. Add the water and mix to a firm dough. Roll out and use to cover the pie. First, dampen edges, place the lid on the pie and press to the edge of dish. Make four cuts out from the centre of the lid, each about 3 inches (7·5 cm.) long. Fold back the triangles of pastry to expose the filling. Decorate with crescent shapes, cut from the pastry trimmings. Brush the pie with beaten egg and bake in a hot oven (425°F., 220°C., Gas Mark 7) for 15 minutes, then reduce the heat to moderate (350°F., 180°C., Gas Mark 4) for a further 30 minutes, until the pastry is crisp and golden brown.

Skibbereen pork crumble

Preparation time 20 minutes
Cooking time 1 hour 30 minutes
Serves 4–6

IMPERIAL/METRIC	AMERICAN
12 oz./350 g. sparerib of pork	¾ lb. sparerib of pork
4 oz./100 g. pig's kidney or liver	¼ lb. pork kidney or liver
¼ pint/1½ dl. chicken stock	⅔ cup chicken stock
salt and pepper to taste	salt and pepper to taste
12 oz./350 g. onions, chopped	3 cups chopped onion
4 oz./100 g. swede or parsnip, chopped	1 cup chopped swede or parsnip
6 oz./175 g. bacon rashers	9 bacon slices
crumble	**crumble**
2 oz./50 g. flour	½ cup all-purpose flour
2 oz./50 g. rolled oats	generous ½ cup rolled oats
2 oz./50 g. butter	¼ cup butter
½ teaspoon powdered sage	½ teaspoon powdered sage

Cut the pork into small thin strips or put through the mincer with the kidney or liver. Place in a saucepan, pour over the stock, season to taste and stir over heat until boiling. Place a layer of vegetables in a greased pie dish, season with salt and pepper. Cover with the meat mixture and more vegetables. Derind the bacon, cut into small pieces and spread on top of the vegetables. Cover the dish and bake in a moderate oven (350°F., 180°C., Gas Mark 4) for about 1 hour. Bake the bacon rinds in an open dish beside the pie until crisp.

To make the crumble, put the flour and oats into a bowl, rub in the butter and mix in the sage. Spread the crumble mixture over the pie and continue cooking for a further 30–35 minutes. Serve the pie topped with crisp bacon rinds.

Note Any cooked, minced meat with vegetables and gravy can be topped with crumble mixture and baked in a moderately hot oven (375°F., 190°C., Gas Mark 5) for 30 minutes.

Rechauffé chicken

Preparation time 15 minutes
Cooking time about 20 minutes
Serves 4

First make the sauce. Chop the tomatoes and deseed and chop the green pepper. Place the olive oil, tomatoes, green pepper, garlic, onion, basil, marjoram, sugar, salt, black pepper and about 6 drops of Tabasco sauce in a saucepan and mix well. Bring to the boil, stirring constantly, and cook until thick. Taste and adjust seasoning carefully. Stir in the tomato purée and wine, and cook for a further 3 minutes. Add the chicken to the sauce and heat through, stirring very gently to avoid breaking up the meat. Pour into a serving dish and sprinkle with chopped parsley. Serve with buttered ribbon noodles.

IMPERIAL/METRIC	AMERICAN
1 lb./450 g. cooked chicken, diced	2 cups diced cooked chicken
sauce	**sauce**
1¼ lb./600 g. tomatoes, peeled	1¼ lb. tomatoes, peeled
1 green pepper	1 green sweet pepper
6 tablespoons olive oil	½ cup olive oil
1 clove garlic, crushed	1 clove garlic, crushed
1 onion, chopped	1 onion, chopped
1 teaspoon dried basil	1 teaspoon dried basil
½ teaspoon dried marjoram	½ teaspoon dried marjoram
1 teaspoon sugar	1 teaspoon sugar
salt and pepper to taste	salt and pepper to taste
Tabasco sauce	Tabasco sauce
1 tablespoon tomato purée	1 tablespoon tomato paste
2 tablespoons white wine	3 tablespoons white wine
1 tablespoon chopped parsley	1 tablespoon chopped parsley

Zesty lamb with dumplings

Preparation time 15 minutes
Cooking time 1 hour 15 minutes
Serves 4

IMPERIAL/METRIC	AMERICAN
½ shoulder of lamb, boned	½ shoulder of lamb, boned
2 tablespoons seasoned flour	3 tablespoons seasoned flour
1 tablespoon oil	1 tablespoon oil
1 large onion, chopped	1 large onion, chopped
1 lb./½ kg. carrots, sliced	1 lb. carrots, sliced
juice of 1 orange	juice of 1 orange
1 chicken stock cube	1 chicken bouillon cube
4 oz./100 g. frozen peas	¾ cup frozen peas
dumplings	**dumplings**
4 oz./100 g. self-raising flour	1 cup all-purpose flour sifted with 1 teaspoon baking powder
2 oz./50 g. shredded suet	scant ½ cup chopped beef suet
finely grated zest of 1 orange	finely grated zest of 1 orange
½ teaspoon dried mixed herbs	½ teaspoon dried mixed herbs
salt and pepper to taste	salt and pepper to taste

Cut the meat into neat pieces and coat in seasoned flour. Heat the oil in a flameproof casserole and use to fry the onion and carrot lightly until softened. Add the meat and fry, stirring, for 2 minutes. Place the orange juice in a measuring jug, add the crumbled stock cube and make up to ¾ pint (½ litre, 2 cups) with boiling water. Pour into the casserole, cover and cook in a moderately hot oven (375°F., 190°C., Gas Mark 5) for 1 hour.

To make the dumplings, place the flour, suet, orange zest, herbs and seasoning in a bowl and mix with enough cold water to give a stiff dough. Knead lightly and form into balls with floured hands. Stir the peas into the casserole and place the dumplings on top of the meat mixture. Replace the cover and return to the oven for a further 15 minutes.

Fricassée of veal

Preparation time 15 minutes
Cooking time 1 hour 30 minutes
Serves 4

IMPERIAL/METRIC	AMERICAN
1½ lb./700 g. pie veal	1½ lb. stewing veal
1 oz./25 g. seasoned flour	¼ cup seasoned flour
1 oz./25 g. butter	2 tablespoons butter
1 large onion, sliced	1 large onion, sliced
1 large carrot, sliced	1 large carrot, sliced
1 tablespoon lemon juice	1 tablespoon lemon juice
½ teaspoon dried rosemary	½ teaspoon dried rosemary
1 (4¾-oz./120-g.) can button mushrooms	1 (4¾-oz.) can button mushrooms
salt and pepper to taste	salt and pepper to taste
3 tablespoons natural yogurt	¼ cup unflavored yogurt
1 tablespoon chopped parsley	1 tablespoon chopped parsley

Dice the meat neatly and coat in seasoned flour. Melt the butter and use to fry the onion and carrot slices gently for 2 minutes, without allowing them to brown. Add the meat and fry quickly on all sides until sealed. Sprinkle in any remaining flour and stir well. Place in an ovenproof casserole and add the lemon juice, rosemary and sufficient water just to cover. Stir and cover. Place in a moderate oven (350°F., 180°C., Gas Mark 4) for 1¼ hours.

Drain the mushrooms and add to the casserole, then adjust the seasoning if necessary. Return to the oven for a further 15 minutes. Remove the lid, stir in the yogurt and serve garnished with parsley.

French bean pot

Preparation time 25 minutes (not including time to soak beans)
Cooking time about 2 hours 10 minutes
Serves 4

IMPERIAL/METRIC	AMERICAN
12 oz./350 g. haricot beans	¾ lb. navy beans
1 large onion	1 large onion
3 cloves	3 cloves
1 lb./450 g. pickled belly of pork	1 lb. fresh picnic shoulder or salt pork
bouquet garni	bouquet garni
1 large clove garlic, crushed	1 large clove garlic, crushed
1 tablespoon bacon dripping or lard	1 tablespoon bacon drippings or lard
1 lb./450 g. pork sausages	1 lb. pork sausages
2 tablespoons tomato purée	3 tablespoons tomato paste
1 teaspoon sugar	1 teaspoon sugar
salt and pepper	salt and pepper
4 tablespoons breadcrumbs (optional)	⅓ cup bread crumbs (optional)

Soak the haricot beans overnight in plenty of cold water. Drain and discard the water. Stick the onion with the cloves and place in a saucepan with the pork, beans, bouquet garni and the garlic. Cover well with warm water and bring to the boil. Cover and simmer gently for 1½ hours or until the beans are tender. Meanwhile, melt the dripping and use to fry the sausages until golden brown all over. Remove and cut each one into 3 or 4 pieces. Add tomato purée to pan with sugar, stir over gentle heat for 3 minutes.

When the beans are cooked, lift out the pork and cut in slices. Remove and dice the rind. Drain the beans, reserving the liquid. Discard the herbs and cloves and chop the onion roughly. Put the beans into a casserole with the diced rind, onion, pork and sausages. Blend ½ pint (3 dl., 1¼ cups) of the reserved stock into the tomato sauce in the frying pan and bring to the boil, stirring constantly. Season to taste and pour the sauce over the beans. Mix well and, if necessary, add a little more stock so the beans are moist but not submerged. If you want a crisp crust, cover the top of the beans with the breadcrumbs. Place the casserole in a moderate oven (350°F., 180°C., Gas Mark 4) for about 40 minutes or until the top is set. Serve with a crusty French loaf.

31

Beef with cheese scone topping

Preparation time 20 minutes
Cooking time about 2 hours
Serves 4

IMPERIAL/METRIC	AMERICAN
2 tablespoons oil	3 tablespoons oil
2 medium onions, chopped	2 medium onions, chopped
1 carrot, sliced	1 carrot, sliced
1¼ lb./600 g. stewing steak, diced	1¼ lb. beef stew meat, diced
1 oz./25 g. flour	¼ cup all-purpose flour
4 tablespoons red wine	⅓ cup red wine
1 beef stock cube	1 beef bouillon cube
1 tablespoon tomato purée	1 tablespoon tomato paste
good pinch sugar	good pinch sugar
1 teaspoon dried marjoram	1 teaspoon dried marjoram
salt and pepper to taste	salt and pepper to taste
scone topping	**scone topping**
8 oz./225 g. self-raising flour	2 cups all-purpose flour sifted with 2 teaspoons baking powder
½ teaspoon dry mustard	½ teaspoon dry mustard
2 oz. strong Cheddar cheese, grated	½ cup grated strong Cheddar cheese
2 oz./50 g. butter	¼ cup butter
¼ pint/1½ dl. milk	⅔ cup milk

Heat the oil and use to fry the onion and carrot until slightly softened. Add the meat and stir over high heat until sealed on all sides. Drain and place in an ovenproof casserole. Add the flour to the remaining fat in the pan and stir until smooth. Place the wine and crumbled stock cube in a measuring jug and make up to ¾ pint (½ litre, 2 cups) with boiling water.

Stir into the pan with the tomato purée, sugar, herbs and seasoning to taste. Bring to the boil, stirring constantly, and pour into the casserole. Cover and cook in a moderate oven (350°F., 180°C., Gas Mark 4) for 1½ hours.

Meanwhile, make the cheese scone topping by placing the dry ingredients in a bowl. Rub in the butter and add sufficient of the milk to make a soft dough. Roll out and cut into fluted rounds. Place these on top of the cooked meat mixture and brush with milk. Raise the oven heat to moderately hot (400°F., 200°C., Gas Mark 6) and return uncovered to the oven for a further 20 minutes.

Limerick lamb

Preparation time 15 minutes
Cooking time about 1 hour 30 minutes
Serves 4–6

IMPERIAL/METRIC	AMERICAN
8 small best end of neck lamb chops or 1½ lb./700 g. middle neck of lamb	8 small lamb rib chops or 1½ lb. neck slices
1 lb./½ kg. onions	1 lb. onions
2 lb./1 kg. potatoes	2 lb. potatoes
salt and pepper to taste	salt and pepper to taste
¾ pint/4 dl. stock	2 cups stock
4 oz./100 g. butter	½ cup butter
2 tablespoons chopped parsley	3 tablespoons chopped parsley
1½ tablespoons Worcestershire sauce	2 tablespoons Worcestershire sauce

Trim any skin and extra fat from the chops or have the middle neck cut in small pieces. Slice the onions thinly and potatoes thickly. Pack layers of vegetables, seasoning and lamb into a wide ovenproof casserole or deep saucepan, making the top layer all potato. Pour in the stock, cover the dish and simmer or bake in a moderate oven (350°F., 180°C., Gas Mark 4) for about 1½ hours. Meanwhile cream the butter until soft and gradually work in the parsley and sauce. Shape into pats and chill them. Serve the stew topped with butter pats or hand them separately.
Note Trimmed off lamb fat can be cooked crisp enough to eat, if put into an open dish or pan alongside the stew.

Farmer's loaf

Preparation time 20 minutes
Cooking time 1 hour 15 minutes
Serves 4

IMPERIAL/METRIC	AMERICAN
1 oz./25 g. lard	2 tablespoons lard
1 onion, chopped	1 onion, chopped
4 sticks celery, chopped	4 stalks celery, chopped
1½ lb./700 g. pork sausagemeat	1½ lb. pork sausagemeat
4 oz./100 g. white breadcrumbs	2 cups white bread crumbs
2 tablespoons chopped parsley	3 tablespoons chopped parsley
salt and pepper to taste	salt and pepper to taste
3 oz./75 g. streaky bacon	4 bacon slices
2 egg yolks	2 egg yolks
¼ pint/1½ dl. milk	⅔ cup milk
sauce	**sauce**
1 oz./25 g. butter	2 tablespoons butter
1 small onion, chopped	1 small onion, chopped
4 oz./100 g. flat mushrooms, peeled and chopped	1 cup peeled and chopped flat mushrooms
½ oz./15 g. flour	2 tablespoons flour
½ pint/3 dl. beef stock	1¼ cups beef stock
salt and pepper to taste	salt and pepper to taste
1 teaspoon soy sauce	1 teaspoon soy sauce
to garnish	**to garnish**
tomato wedges and parsley	tomato wedges and parsley

Melt the lard and fry the onion and celery gently for 5 minutes. Mix together with the sausagemeat, breadcrumbs, parsley and seasoning. Derind the bacon and stretch with the back of a knife. Use to line the base of a greased 2-lb. (1-kg.) loaf tin and press down well. Mix together the yolks and milk and stir into the sausagemeat mixture. Turn the mixture into the loaf tin, press down and smooth the top. Cover with foil and stand the tin in a bain marie. Bake in a moderate oven (350°F., 180°C., Gas Mark 4) for about 1 hour 15 minutes.

To make the sauce, melt the butter in a saucepan and fry the onion gently for 5 minutes. Add the mushrooms and fry for a further 3 minutes. Stir in the flour, remove from the heat and blend in the stock. Bring to the boil, stirring, and simmer gently for 1 minute. Season well and add the soy sauce. Turn the loaf on to a warm serving dish, garnish with tomato wedges and parsley and hand the sauce separately.

Beef Valencia

Preparation time 25 minutes plus soaking time for prunes
Cooking time about 1 hour 15 minutes
Serves 4

IMPERIAL/METRIC	AMERICAN
2 oz./50 g. prunes, soaked overnight	⅓ cup prunes, soaked overnight
1½ lb./700 g. stewing steak	1½ lb. beef stew meat
1 oz./25 g. seasoned cornflour	¼ cup seasoned cornstarch
2 tablespoons corn oil	3 tablespoons corn oil
1 onion, chopped	1 onion, chopped
1 clove garlic, crushed	1 clove garlic, crushed
2 oranges	2 oranges
¼ pint/1½ dl. cider	⅔ cup cider
2 beef stock cubes	2 beef bouillon cubes
few olives	few olives

Soak the prunes overnight in cold water. Trim the meat and cut into cubes, then coat with the seasoned cornflour. Heat the corn oil and use to sauté the meat, onion and garlic, until onion is golden. Thinly peel the zest from one orange. Squeeze the juice from both, add to the cider and make the quantity up to 1 pint (6 dl., 2½ cups) with water. Blanch the zest from the orange in boiling water for a few minutes, drain and cut into shreds. Add half the zest to the meat and vegetables and reserve the rest for the garnish. Add the beef stock cubes and the 1 pint (6 dl., 2½ cups) liquid. Stir well and bring to the boil. Cover and simmer gently for 45 minutes.

Stone the prunes and stuff each one with an olive, then put into the saucepan and continue cooking for a further 20–30 minutes or until the meat is tender. Sprinkle the orange shreds on top to garnish.

Monday hash

Preparation time 20–25 minutes
Cooking time 40 minutes
Serves 4

IMPERIAL/METRIC	AMERICAN
1 oz./25 g. dripping	2 tablespoons drippings
8 oz./225 g. minced beef	1 cup ground beef
1 small onion, chopped	1 small onion, chopped
2 oz./50 g. mushrooms, sliced	½ cup sliced mushrooms
8 oz./225 g. cooked lamb or pork, minced	1 cup ground cooked lamb or pork
few drops Tabasco sauce	few drops Tabasco sauce
½ pint/3 dl. gravy	1¼ cups brown stock
salt and pepper to taste	salt and pepper to taste
1 lb./½ kg. potatoes	1 lb. potatoes
2 oz./50 g. butter	¼ cup butter
1 tablespoon oil	1 tablespoon oil

Melt half the dripping and use to fry the minced beef until it changes colour, stirring frequently. Drain and place in an ovenproof casserole. Add the remaining dripping to the pan and use it to fry the onion and mushrooms, until the onion is just pale golden brown. Drain, reserve a few mushroom slices for the garnish, and add to the casserole with the cooked meat, Tabasco, gravy and seasoning. Mix well together and smooth the surface.

Meanwhile, cook the potatoes until tender and mash with the butter. Pile on top of the meat mixture and rough up the surface with a fork. Brush with oil and place the casserole in a moderately hot oven (400°F., 200°C., Gas Mark 6) for 40 minutes. Garnish with the reserved mushroom slices and return to the oven for a further 4 minutes. Serve with vegetables in season.

Cream-crusted beef

Preparation time 15 minutes
Cooking time 30 minutes
Serves 4–6

IMPERIAL/METRIC	AMERICAN
2 oz./50 g. dripping	¼ cup drippings
1 large onion, chopped	1 large onion, chopped
1 tablespoon tomato purée	1 tablespoon tomato paste
salt and pepper to taste	salt and pepper to taste
1½ lb./700 g. minced beef	1½ lb. ground beef
½ pint/3 dl. beef stock	1¼ cups beef stock
8 oz./225 g. mushrooms, sliced	2 cups sliced mushrooms
2 eggs	2 eggs
1 (5-oz./150-g.) carton soured cream	1 (5-oz.) carton sour cream
½ teaspoon paprika pepper	½ teaspoon paprika pepper

Melt half the dripping in a frying pan, add the onion and cook gently until limp but not coloured. Stir in the tomato purée and seasoning. Add the minced beef and cook over medium heat for about 3 minutes, stirring constantly. Add enough stock to keep the mixture moist and place in an ovenproof casserole. Melt the remaining dripping and fry the mushrooms very lightly. Sprinkle with salt and pepper and place on top of the meat. Beat the eggs into the soured cream, add the paprika and a little salt. Pour this mixture over the casserole and bake in a moderate oven (350°F., 180°C., Gas Mark 4) for about 30 minutes until the topping is set and golden.

Savoury mince parcels

ILLUSTRATED IN COLOUR ON PAGE 20
Preparation time 25–30 minutes
Cooking time about 1 hour 15 minutes
Serves 4

IMPERIAL/METRIC	AMERICAN
1 small onion	1 small onion
2 oz./50 g. mushrooms	½ cup mushrooms
½ oz./15 g. lard	1 tablespoon lard
8 oz./225 g. minced beef	1 cup ground beef
½ oz./15 g. plain flour	2 tablespoons all-purpose flour
¼ pint/1½ dl. beef stock	⅔ cup beef stock
1 teaspoon made mustard	1 teaspoon prepared mustard
1 tablespoon tomato purée	1 tablespoon tomato paste
pinch mixed herbs	pinch mixed herbs
salt and pepper	salt and pepper
8 oz./225 g. sausagemeat	½ lb. sausagemeat
12 oz./350 g. shortcrust pastry mix	¾ lb. pie crust mix
6–8 tablespoons milk	about ½ cup milk
1 egg, beaten	1 egg, beaten

Finely chop the onion and mushrooms. Melt the lard in a saucepan and use to gently fry the onion and mushrooms until tender. Add the minced beef and brown lightly all over. Stir in the flour and cook for a minute. Remove from heat and gradually stir in stock, mustard, tomato purée, herbs and seasoning. Return to the heat and bring to the boil, stirring. Cook gently for 5 minutes, stirring occasionally. Remove from the heat and mix in the sausagemeat. Leave the mixture until cold.

Put the pastry mix into a bowl and add enough milk to mix to a fairly stiff dough. Roll out on a floured board to a large square and cut into four 6½-inch (16-cm.) squares. Divide the meat mixture into four and pile in the centre of each square of pastry. Moisten the edges of the pastry with water and draw the edges up into the centre to form an envelope shape. Press the edges well together and crimp as for Cornish pasties. Place on a greased baking sheet, brush with beaten egg and bake in a moderately hot oven (400°F., 200°C., Gas Mark 6) for 30 minutes. Reduce the heat to moderate (350°F., 180°C., Gas Mark 4) and continue cooking for a further 20–30 minutes, or until golden brown and filling is tender.

Caraway beef casserole

Preparation time 10 minutes
Cooking time 1 hour 20 minutes
Serves 4

IMPERIAL/METRIC	AMERICAN
1½ lb./700 g. white cabbage	1½ lb. white cabbage
1 tablespoon oil	1 tablespoon oil
2 teaspoons caraway seeds	2 teaspoons caraway seeds
8 oz./225 g. potatoes, sliced	½ lb. potatoes, sliced
1 lb./450 g. minced beef	2 cups ground beef
salt and pepper to taste	salt and pepper to taste
1 beef stock cube	1 beef bouillon cube
¼ pint/1½ dl. boiling water	⅔ cup boiling water
8 oz./225 g. tomatoes, halved	½ lb. tomatoes, halved

Shred the cabbage, discarding any hard core. Place the oil in the base of a large flameproof casserole. Add a third of the cabbage, caraway seeds, potato and meat. Season well. Make up strong stock with the cube and water, pour a third over. Repeat the process twice more, ending with a layer of cabbage and pour over the remaining stock. Bring to the boil, cover the pan and simmer for 1 hour. Add the tomato halves, cut sides upwards round the edge of the pan. Re-cover and cook for a further 20 minutes.

Creative
flower arrangements

Flowers, whether a single perfect bloom or a riot of colour, give a special welcome to your guests. My own collection of containers is carefully cherished, including an outsize breakfast cup, just right for primroses and anemones from my rockery. If the container is the right shape and depth, the completed arrangement can be placed inside a shallow woven basket, china plant pot holder, or even a decorative soup tureen, with considerable effect. A Victorian teapot which was broken, carefully stuck together but not leakproof, is my favourite holder for a jam jar filled with old-fashioned cottage garden flowers; forget-me-nots, nasturtiums and Michaelmas daisies in turn. No-one need be deterred from attempting professional looking arrangements by the lack of bowls and urns or elegant vases.

Treatment of flowers

Flowers, which often give a sensational effect when arranged, need careful treatment beforehand if they are not to wilt within a few hours. So let us begin with the right treatment to preserve cut flowers as long as

possible. Wild and garden blooms should never be left lying in the sun but placed straight into large polythene bags, or made into bunches wrapped with damp newspaper around the stems, each bunch enclosed in a foil holder.

Soft-stemmed flowers should be chosen in bud if possible. Trim an inch from the stems at a slanting angle and plunge the flowers into a bucket of water, at room temperature, as far up the stems as possible. Flowers like tulips, which droop easily, enjoy the addition of a pinch of sugar to the water. One can even insert a plastic drinking straw up the stem. Woody stems need an inch-long slit up the centre or crushing to make it easier for the stem ends to absorb water. This is how I treat chrysanthemums and roses. Hollow-stemmed flowers like lupins stand up well if you invert the flower head and fill the stem with water. Keep your thumb over the filled stem until you get it back into water and trim to length *under* water. Some flowers bleed a milky liquid and you can prevent this by sealing the stem ends in a flame, making sure the flower head is held well away. Strip off all base leaves that will be completely submerged.

Equipment and containers

Anyone who has spent an irritating half hour trying to arrange floppy-stemmed flowers in a bowl will appreciate that a few simple accessories make all the difference to easy and successful displays. Strong kitchen scissors with serrated edges are needed to cut woody stems and wire mesh. The latter is useful, crumpled loosely into a ball, to fit the shape of the vase. A few ends of cut wire can be left poking out to bend over the rim of the vase and hold the ball steady. Pin-holders, which range from the tiny $\frac{1}{2}$-inch (1-cm.) size to a 5-inch (13-cm.) circular porcupine, are equally useful but tend to shift a bit in use. Some have suction pads but if yours have none, try putting a bed of plasticine into the dry container first and then press the pin-holder down on to it. Florists' wire holds flower stems and twigs in a bent position. Pins or green twist ties are also helpful. I often use blocks of damped absorbent plastic foam to make my arrangement, then fill up with water.

All-round and facing arrangements

There are basically two types of arrangement which particularly interest the hostess.

All-round This is used as the centrepiece of a table, with guests all round who will see it from every angle. It should be low so that it does not interrupt the view across the table. The shape should harmonise with the shape of the table and ought not to dominate it. A round container looks well with a large tapering candle in the centre. Fix a low candle holder in place with plasticine before surrounding with mesh or plastic foam for the flowers, and arrange them to cover this completely. Place the tallest central flowers first (to prevent you from building up more height than you need). Then establish the shape round the edge of the container with a number of almost horizontal outline points of trailing ivy, flexible leafy twigs or natural foliage from the flowers, then fill in the shape like a shallow cone. A delicate shoot of trailing ivy can be twisted up round the candle and secured near the point with a short pin or bent staple. The candle could be replaced by a central tall flower. A pair of candle-sticks can then be used either side of the flower arrangement on a rectangular table. The same type of arrangement can be used for a trough with trailers at either end, if the table is a long one.

Facing On a buffet table, against the wall or for any arrangement which can be seen from one side only, the facing style permits quite an imposing flower display without being too extravagant with materials. It is best to aim for a total height three times the depth of the basic container, giving a sort of uneven triangular effect. Place the tallest and widest flowers slightly behind the centre of the vase. Fill in the outline avoiding a rigid triangular shape. Place some large eye-catching flowers with leaves fairly low in the front and fill in the outline so that a balanced shape is achieved, to be seen only from the sides and front, so that the back third of the vase is left almost empty. Odd, short pieces of greenery etc. can be tucked in so that there is no impression of emptiness. Don't be afraid to use unusual materials such as dried seed pods and grasses.

Perfect answers to the teatime problem

Tea, as a meal, seems to mean different things to different people. For children it is probably the last meal of the day and has to be fairly substantial, even if guests are invited. For office workers, who have existed on sandwiches and a cardboard carton of coffee at lunch time, it also needs to be more of a meal. The wait for a formal dinner would be agonising! Yet it may suggest to others rather an elegant occasion with embroidered tablecloth, silver teapot and dainty little cakes.

In this chapter I have tried to cover the whole gamut of teatime catering. Children and others who rush out early without time for breakfast, appreciate the bacon and eggs they missed in the morning, made up into savoury dishes. Potato cakes with bacon and egg or Cheese and bacon scones would be quite a treat.

Unusual home-made tea breads are family favourites, which send your children's school friends home demanding that their mothers make the same. Since buttermilk has become easier to obtain, I particularly like Irish buttermilk bread. Other home-baked breads may be sweet or savoury, served spread with butter or eaten with cheese and fruit – a healthy meal for growing youngsters.

Sandwiches, if nicely trimmed, make an average teatable look more like a party. Put slices of white and brown bread together and arrange the sandwiches alternate sides up, to give the chequered effect. The well known fillings get boring so use something you haven't tried before. I recently discovered that corned beef mashed with apricot chutney is extremely tasty (see picture). Try seasoned cream cheese with plenty of chopped watercress folded in, lemon curd mixed with mashed banana, or peanut butter with beetroot and cucumber.

If you have a really fresh white sandwich loaf, make pinwheels – you can see how they look in the colour photograph on page 96. Remove the crust all along one side, butter lightly and very carefully cut one long slice from the loaf, trim off the crusts. Place a row of stuffed olives all along one long edge, spreading the rest of the surface with a pretty pink fish paste, or canned dressed crab. Turn the edge with the olives over and roll up tightly to the opposite side. Wrap closely in foil or cling film and chill until firm. Even freeze the rolls, with suitable wrapping, and partially defrost when required to serve. Slice thinly and arrange while still very cold as they are rather hard to handle, and tend to unroll.

Cakes, of course, are the standby of every festive tea. Here you will find a wide choice, from an impressive iced gâteau to a simple Spring ring cake. Small cakes can be made to look extremely decorative. My family voted Coconut truffles an instant success.

Ice cream always makes a welcome appearance. Not just vanilla by any means; scoops of lime and lemon ice cream, such a pretty pale green colour, quickly becomes exciting when you melt lime flavoured boiled sweets in very little water and pour it over while still hot. This sets into a crunchy topping; different flavoured sweets could be used in the same way.

Salmon and egg savouries (page 41), fried smoked oysters and mushrooms (page 40), sandwiches filled with corned beef and apricot chutney, and apricot layer desserts (page 48).

Savoury fish pie

Preparation time 25 minutes
Cooking time 40 minutes
Serves 4–6

IMPERIAL/METRIC	AMERICAN
12 oz./350 g. smoked haddock	¾ lb. smoked haddock
¼ pint/1½ dl. milk	⅔ cup milk
3 eggs	3 eggs
8 oz./225 g. cheese, grated	2 cups grated cheese
salt and pepper	salt and pepper
shake cayenne pepper	shake cayenne pepper
2 tablespoons cream (optional)	3 tablespoons cream (optional)
shortcrust pastry	**shortcrust pastry**
4 oz./100 g. mixture of cooking fat and hard margarine	½ cup mixture of shortening and lard
8 oz./225 g. plain flour	2 cups all-purpose flour
pinch salt	pinch salt
3–4 tablespoons water	4–5 tablespoons water

Put the haddock in a flameproof casserole with the milk and poach in the oven or on top of the cooker for about 10–15 minutes, then allow to cool. Hard-boil 2 eggs and beat up the third egg.

Make the pastry by rubbing the fat into the sieved flour and salt. Mix with water and roll out on a floured board. Line an 8-inch (20-cm.) flan ring with two-thirds of the pastry.

Drain the fish from the milk and flake into a bowl, removing any bones. Add the cheese, salt, pepper, cayenne, chopped eggs and the milk and cream mixed with most of the beaten egg. Put the mixture into the flan ring and wet the pastry surface with water. Roll out the remaining third of the pastry and cover the top of the ring. Seal the edges with the prongs of a fork and make three slits on the top. Brush with beaten egg and bake in a moderately hot oven (400°F., 200°C., Gas Mark 6) for 40 minutes. Serve with grilled tomatoes.

Potato cake grill

Preparation time 10 minutes
Cooking time 10 minutes
Serves 4

IMPERIAL/METRIC	AMERICAN
1 lb./450 g. boiled potatoes	1 lb. boiled potatoes
1 small egg	1 egg
salt and pepper	salt and pepper
2 tablespoons flour	3 tablespoons flour
4 rashers bacon	4 bacon slices
4 eggs	4 eggs

Sieve the potatoes into a bowl, make a well in the centre and add the egg, salt and pepper and sieved flour, mixing well all the time. Turn on to a floured board and roll out to about ¼ inch (0·5 cm.) thick. Cut into 2½-inch (6·5-cm.) rounds or triangles and cook in batches on a greased griddle or non-stick frying pan. Grill the bacon rashers while the potato cakes are cooking and lastly fry the eggs.

Fried smoked oysters and mushrooms

ILLUSTRATED IN COLOUR ON PAGE 39
Preparation time 10 minutes
Cooking time about 5 minutes
Serves 4

IMPERIAL/METRIC	AMERICAN
8 oz./225 g. button mushrooms	2 cups button mushrooms
2 (3¾-oz./100-g.) cans smoked oysters	2 (3¾-oz.) cans smoked oysters
2 tablespoons vinegar	3 tablespoons vinegar
1 egg, beaten	1 egg, beaten
¼ pint/1½ dl. milk	⅔ cup milk
seasoned flour	seasoned flour
corn oil for frying	corn oil for frying

Trim off the mushroom stalks. Drain the oysters well and rinse in a little vinegar to remove the oil, then rinse in water to remove the vinegar. Dry on absorbent kitchen paper. Beat together the egg and milk, coat the oysters and mushrooms in the milk mixture then in seasoned flour. Either shallow fry in oil over a fairly high heat for 2 minutes each side, until golden brown. Or, deep fry in very hot oil for 3–4 minutes. Drain well and serve hot with hot buttered toast.

Cheese and bacon scones

Preparation time 15 minutes
Cooking time 15–20 minutes
Serves 4

IMPERIAL/METRIC	AMERICAN
4 rashers lean bacon	4 bacon slices or Canadian bacon slices
8 oz./225 g. plain flour	2 cups all-purpose flour
pinch salt	pinch salt
1 teaspoon baking powder	1 teaspoon baking powder
$\frac{1}{4}$ teaspoon dry mustard	$\frac{1}{4}$ teaspoon dry mustard
2 oz./50 g. butter or margarine	$\frac{1}{4}$ cup butter or margarine
1½ oz./40 g. cheese, grated	$\frac{1}{3}$ cup grated cheese
1 egg	1 egg
$\frac{1}{4}$ pint/1½ dl. sour milk	$\frac{2}{3}$ cup sour milk
4 rashers streaky bacon	4 bacon slices
to garnish	**to garnish**
watercress	watercress

Cut the rind from the bacon and grill or fry until crisp. Crumble or cut into small pieces. Sieve the flour, salt, baking powder and dry mustard into a bowl then rub in the butter until the mixture resembles fine crumbs. Add 1 tablespoon of grated cheese and the bacon pieces. Make a well in the centre of the mixture and pour in the egg and sour milk. Mix from the centre outwards until the mixture forms one lump. Turn on to a floured board and knead lightly. Form or roll into a round about 7–8 inches (18–20 cm.) in diameter and cut into 8 wedges. Brush with milk, sprinkle with the remaining grated cheese and bake in a moderately hot oven (400°F., 200°C., Gas Mark 6) until golden brown, about 15–20 minutes.

Make small bacon rolls with the remaining bacon, arrange on a baking tray and cook in the oven with the scones for at least 10 minutes. Serve in the centre of the scones, and garnish with watercress.

Salmon and egg savouries

ILLUSTRATED IN COLOUR ON PAGE 39
Preparation time 5 minutes
Cooking time 10 minutes
Serves 4

IMPERIAL/METRIC	AMERICAN
1½ oz./40 g. butter	3 tablespoons butter
2 tablespoons oil	3 tablespoons oil
4 slices bread, trimmed	4 slices bread, trimmed
1 small onion, chopped	1 small onion, chopped
1 (7½-oz./215-g.) can pink salmon	1 (7½-oz.) can pink salmon
4 eggs	4 eggs
1 tablespoon chopped parsley	1 tablespoon chopped parsley

Heat together the butter and oil and use to fry the bread slices on both sides, until golden brown. Remove and keep hot. Add the onion to the remaining fat in the pan and cook gently until soft but not coloured. Stir in the flaked salmon and liquid from the can, reheat gently. Meanwhile, poach the eggs. Divide the salmon mixture between the four slices of bread and smooth with a knife. Top each one with a poached egg and garnish with a sprinkling of chopped parsley. Serve hot.

Savoury sausage fries

Preparation time 15 minutes
Cooking time 20 minutes
Serves 4

IMPERIAL/METRIC	AMERICAN
12 oz./350 g. pork sausagemeat	¾ lb. pork sausagemeat
2 heaped tablespoons sage and onion stuffing	3 heaped tablespoons sage and onion stuffing
few drops Worcestershire sauce	few drops Worcestershire sauce
salt and pepper to taste	salt and pepper to taste
2 eggs, lightly beaten	2 eggs, lightly beaten
breadcrumbs for coating	bread crumbs for coating
oil for frying	oil for frying
1 bunch watercress	1 bunch watercress
sauce	**sauce**
1 large onion	1 large onion
1 tablespoon oil	1 tablespoon oil
1 (10-oz./275-g.) can peeled tomatoes	1 (10-oz.) can peeled tomatoes
½ teaspoon sugar	½ teaspoon sugar
few drops Worcestershire sauce	few drops Worcestershire sauce
1 tablespoon tomato purée	1 tablespoon tomato paste
salt and pepper	salt and pepper
½ teaspoon dried herbs	½ teaspoon dried herbs
2 tablespoons stock or water	3 tablespoons stock or water

Mix together the sausagemeat, dry stuffing, seasoning and half the beaten egg. Add enough hot water to make a firm paste. Allow to stand for at least 10 minutes.

Meanwhile, make the sauce by frying the finely chopped onion in the oil until transparent. Add all other ingredients and cook for 15 minutes, then liquidise in a blender or sieve into a sauce boat.

Divide the pork mixture into 12 even-sized balls. Coat in remaining egg and breadcrumbs. Deep fry (or shallow fry on both sides) in oil until rich golden brown. Serve with the sauce and garnish with watercress.

Orange-egg curry

Preparation time 15 minutes
Cooking time 15–20 minutes
Serves 4–6

IMPERIAL/METRIC	AMERICAN
1 oz./25 g. butter	2 tablespoons butter
2 tablespoons chopped onion	3 tablespoons chopped onion
2 tablespoons flour	3 tablespoons all-purpose flour
1 teaspoon curry powder	1 teaspoon curry powder
½ pint/3 dl. milk	1¼ cups milk
½ teaspoon salt	½ teaspoon salt
pinch pepper	pinch pepper
2 teaspoons grated orange rind	2 teaspoons grated orange rind
juice of 1 orange	juice of 1 orange
6 hard-boiled eggs	6 hard-cooked eggs
6 oz./175 g. rice, cooked	scant 1 cup rice, cooked
chopped parsley	chopped parsley

Melt the butter in a saucepan, add the chopped onion and cook until transparent. Blend in the flour and curry powder until smooth, and cook until the mixture bubbles. Add the milk slowly and continue to cook, stirring constantly, until thickened. Next add the salt, pepper, orange rind and juice and five of the quartered hard-boiled eggs. Reserve the sixth egg for garnishing. Heat the mixture, stirring gently to avoid breaking the eggs. Turn the hot, cooked rice into an oval dish, and serve the curry spooned on the top. Garnish with the remaining quartered egg. Sprinkle with parsley.

Irish buttermilk bread

Preparation time 10 minutes
Cooking time about 35 minutes
Serves 4

IMPERIAL/METRIC	AMERICAN
12 oz./350 g. wholewheat flour	3 cups whole-grain flour
4 oz./100 g. self-raising flour	1 cup all-purpose flour sifted with 1 teaspoon baking powder
1 teaspoon salt	1 teaspoon salt
½ teaspoon bicarbonate of soda	½ teaspoon baking soda
2 oz./50 g. butter	¼ cup butter
½ pint/3 dl. buttermilk	1¼ cups buttermilk

Put the dry ingredients into a bowl, rub in the butter and mix with buttermilk to make a firm dough. Knead lightly to tuck in the rough edges and pat into a round about 1½ inches (4 cm.) deep. Put on to a baking sheet, dusted with wholewheat flour, and make four deep cross cuts into the dough. Bake in a moderately hot oven (400°F., 200°C., Gas Mark 6) for 35–40 minutes, until the bread is well risen and browned. Break the wedges apart and serve cold with plenty of butter, cheese or honey.

Cottage cheese and celery teabread

Preparation time 15 minutes
Cooking time 40–45 minutes
Serves 6–8

IMPERIAL/METRIC	AMERICAN
1 (8-oz./225-g.) carton cottage cheese, sieved	1 cup sieved cottage cheese
4 oz./100 g. soft brown sugar	½ cup soft brown sugar
3 eggs	3 eggs
2 oz./50 g. mixed nuts, chopped	½ cup chopped mixed nuts
2 sticks celery, chopped	2 stalks celery, chopped
8 oz./225 g. self-raising flour	2 cups all-purpose flour sifted with 3 teaspoons baking powder
1 teaspoon baking powder	

Cream together the cottage cheese and sugar, then beat in the eggs. Stir in the nuts and celery. Sift together the flour and baking powder and fold into the mixture. Line a 2-lb. (1-kg.) loaf tin with grease-proof paper and brush with oil. Spoon in the mixture and bake in a moderate oven (350°F., 180°C., Gas Mark 4) for 40–45 minutes until risen and browned. Leave for 5 minutes in the tin, then remove, peel off the greaseproof paper and cool. Serve sliced with butter.

Shamrock cream crackers

Preparation time 10 minutes
Cooking time 2 minutes
Serves 4

IMPERIAL/METRIC	AMERICAN
8 oz./225 g. Cheddar cheese	½ lb. Cheddar cheese
8 oz./225 g. butter	1 cup butter
freshly ground pepper	freshly ground pepper
4 tablespoons buttermilk	⅓ cup buttermilk
12 cream crackers	12 (3-inch square) crackers
topping	**topping**
2 oz./50 g. almonds, chopped	½ cup chopped almonds
1 oz./25 g. butter	2 tablespoons butter
salt	salt
to garnish	**to garnish**
cress	cress

Grate the cheese finely and beat thoroughly into the butter with pepper to taste. Add the buttermilk to make a spreading mixture.

Chop the almonds roughly. Melt the butter in a pan and use to fry the almonds until they are golden brown. Drain them and sprinkle liberally with salt. Spread the cheese on the crackers, top with the almonds and garnish with small bunches of cress, pressed into the edges of the cheese mixture.

Chapel windows

Preparation time 30 minutes
Cooking time 35–45 minutes

IMPERIAL/METRIC	AMERICAN
3 eggs	3 eggs
5 oz./125 g. castor sugar	⅔ cup sugar
¼ teaspoon vanilla essence	¼ teaspoon vanilla extract
3 oz./75 g. self-raising flour	¾ cup all-purpose flour sifted with ¾ teaspoon baking powder
1 oz./25 g. butter	2 tablespoons butter
red food colouring	red food coloring
covering	**covering**
8 oz./225 g. almond paste	½ lb. almond paste
2 tablespoons sieved apricot jam	3 tablespoons sieved apricot jam
to decorate	**to decorate**
glacé cherries and pineapple	candied cherries and pineapple

Grease and line a 7-inch (18-cm.) square tin. Divide the tin into two compartments by placing a piece of greaseproof paper down the centre. Put the eggs and castor sugar in a basin over hot water and beat until thick and creamy. Alternatively, an electric mixer will beat the mixture thickly enough without whisking over the water. Add the vanilla essence and gradually sieve in the flour, folding gently with a metal spoon or spatula. Lastly fold the melted but cooled butter into the mixture. Pour half the mixture into one side of the tin. Colour the other half of the mixture by carefully folding in a few drops of red colouring. Pour the pink mixture into the other side of the tin and bake in a moderate oven (350°F., 180°C., Gas Mark 4) for 35–45 minutes. Turn out and cool on a wire tray.

Trim the cakes and cut each into two even-sized lengths. Sandwich together with the sieved jam, alternating the colours.

Brush the outside edge of the cake with warmed sieved jam. Roll the almond paste into a rectangle, using icing sugar to prevent it sticking to the rolling pin. When it is the same size as the cake, wrap it around the cake and seal well. Make a criss cross pattern on the top and flute the edges. Decorate with glacé cherries and pineapple.

The same cake can be made in a Swiss roll tin, dividing the mixture into three and colouring the sponge green and pink. The colours are then alternated to make six squares instead of four.

Walnut and orange loaf

Preparation time 20 minutes
Cooking time 1–1 hour 15 minutes

IMPERIAL/METRIC	AMERICAN
8 oz./225 g. plain flour	2 cups all-purpose flour
pinch salt	pinch salt
1 teaspoon baking powder	1 teaspoon baking powder
4 oz./100 g. margarine	½ cup margarine
4 oz./100 g. castor sugar	½ cup sugar
4 oz./100 g. shelled walnuts	1 cup walnuts
1 large or 2 small oranges	1 large or 2 small oranges
1 egg	1 egg
little milk	little milk

Grease a 1-lb. (½-kg.) loaf tin. Sieve the flour, salt and baking powder into a basin. Rub in the margarine until the mixture is like fine crumbs. Stir in the sugar and chopped walnuts. Grate the rind of the orange and squeeze the juice (should yield at least 3 tablespoons). Add the orange rind to the mixture, make a well in the centre and add the egg and the orange juice. Mix to a dropping consistency by adding a little milk if the mixture is too stiff. Bake in a moderate oven (350°F., 180°C., Gas Mark 4) for 1–1¼ hours. Serve buttered.

Spring ring cake

Preparation time 10–15 minutes
Cooking time 20 minutes

IMPERIAL/METRIC	AMERICAN
2 oz./50 g. castor sugar	¼ cup sugar
2 eggs	2 eggs
1 oz./25 g. butter	2 tablespoons butter
2 oz./50 g. plain flour	½ cup all-purpose flour
grated rind of 1 lemon	grated rind of 1 lemon
icing	**icing**
6 oz./175 g. icing sugar	1⅓ cups sifted confectioners' sugar
2 tablespoons lemon juice	3 tablespoons lemon juice

Place the sugar and eggs in a bowl over a pan of hot water and whisk until thick and pale in colour. Remove from the heat and whisk until cooled. Melt the butter and gradually fold in with the sieved flour and lemon rind.

Pour into a 7-inch (18-cm.) greased and floured ring tin. Bake in a preheated moderately hot oven (375°F., 190°C., Gas Mark 5) for 20 minutes. Turn out carefully on to a wire tray and cool.

To make the icing, mix the icing sugar and lemon juice together and allow it to dribble down the sides of the cake.

Dark chocolate gâteau

Preparation time 30 minutes
Cooking time 40–45 minutes

IMPERIAL/METRIC	AMERICAN
3 eggs	3 eggs
4½ oz./125 g. castor sugar	½ cup plus 1 tablespoon sugar
1 oz./25 g. cocoa powder	¼ cup unsweetened cocoa powder
5 tablespoons hot water	6 tablespoons hot water
1 oz./25 g. cooking chocolate	1 square cooking chocolate
2¼ oz./60 g. self-raising flour	½ cup plus 1 tablespoon all-purpose flour sifted with ½ teaspoon baking powder
filling and topping	**filling and topping**
½ pint/3 dl. double cream	1¼ cups whipping cream
2 oz./50 g. castor sugar	¼ cup sugar
few drops vanilla essence	few drops vanilla extract
to decorate	**to decorate**
cherries (or other fruit)	cherries (or other fruit)
glacé or canned pineapple pieces	candied or canned pineapple pieces

Prepare an 8-inch (20-cm.) loose bottomed cake tin by brushing with oil and dusting with flour. Beat the eggs and sugar together until thick and creamy, either with an electric mixer or put the bowl over hot water if using a hand mixer. Mix the cocoa powder and water together, melt the chocolate in a bowl over hot water and gradually mix with the cocoa mixture. Allow to cool. Sieve the flour, then add about two-thirds to the thick egg mixture. Blend in the chocolate and the remaining flour. Pour into the prepared tin and bake in a moderate oven (350°F., 180°C., Gas Mark 4) for 40–45 minutes. Turn out to cool on a wire rack.

Split the cake into three. Lightly whip the double cream until just thick. Beat in the sugar and vanilla essence. Spread some of the cream over the bottom two rounds of the cake and restack together. Spread cream over the top. Put the remaining cream into a piping bag with a large star pipe. Pipe all over the sides. Decorate with cherries and candied or canned pineapple pieces.

Marshmallow frosted cake

Preparation time 15–20 minutes
Cooking time 30 minutes

IMPERIAL/METRIC	AMERICAN
4 oz./100 g. butter	½ cup butter
8 oz./225 g. castor sugar	1 cup sugar
2 oz./50 g. brown sugar	¼ cup brown sugar
3 eggs	3 eggs
1 teaspoon vanilla essence	1 teaspoon vanilla extract
2 oz./50 g. plain chocolate	2 oz. semi-sweet chocolate
8 oz./225 g. plain flour	2 cups all-purpose flour
1 teaspoon bicarbonate of soda	1 teaspoon baking soda
½ teaspoon salt	½ teaspoon salt
¼ pint/1½ dl. buttermilk	⅔ cup buttermilk
marshmallow frosting	**marshmallow frosting**
6 oz./175 g. marshmallows	6 oz. marshmallows
2 tablespoons milk	3 tablespoons milk
1 egg white	1 egg white
1 oz./25 g. castor sugar	2 tablespoons sugar
to decorate	**to decorate**
chocolate vermicelli	chocolate vermicelli

Cream the butter and sugar well. Separate the eggs and add the yolks, one by one, to the creamed mixture. Melt the chocolate in a bowl over a saucepan of hot water and blend into the creamed mixture. Sieve the flour, bicarbonate of soda and salt together and fold into the mixture alternately with the buttermilk. Whisk the egg whites until stiff and fold into the cake mixture. Divide the mixture equally between 2 well greased 8-inch (20-cm.) sandwich tins. Bake in the centre of a moderate oven (350°F., 180°C., Gas Mark 4) for 30 minutes. Turn out and cool on a wire tray.

Make the marshmallow frosting by melting the marshmallows slowly in the milk. Leave to cool, stirring occasionally. Beat the egg white and sugar until stiff and peaky, fold into the marshmallow. Allow to set a little.

Use to fill the centre of the cake and coat the top and sides. Sprinkle a little chocolate vermicelli on the top.

Kolac

Preparation time 20 minutes
Cooking time 35–40 minutes
Makes 24

IMPERIAL/METRIC	AMERICAN
8 oz./225 g. wholemeal flour	2 cups whole-grain flour
2 teaspoons baking powder	2 teaspoons baking powder
¼ teaspoon salt	¼ teaspoon salt
4 oz./100 g. butter	½ cup butter
3 oz./75 g. soft brown sugar	6 tablespoons soft brown sugar
1 egg, beaten	1 egg, beaten
2 dessert apples, cored and sliced	2 eating apples, cored and sliced
2 bananas, sliced	2 bananas, sliced
12 oz./350 g. cottage cheese, sieved	1½ cups sieved cottage cheese
2 oz./50 g. soft brown sugar	¼ cup soft brown sugar
½ oz./15 g. butter	1 tablespoon butter

Mix together flour, baking powder and salt. Rub in the butter until the mixture resembles fine breadcrumbs. Stir in the soft brown sugar and mix to a stiff dough with beaten egg. Roll out and use to line a greased 13 × 9-inch (34 × 23-cm.) Swiss roll tin. Spread the apple and banana evenly over the pastry and top with cottage cheese. Sprinkle with soft brown sugar and dot with butter. Bake in a moderately hot oven (375°F., 190°C., Gas Mark 5) for 35–40 minutes. Cool and cut into 2-inch (5-cm.) squares.

Coconut truffles

Preparation time 15 minutes
Makes 12–16

IMPERIAL/METRIC	AMERICAN
2 oz./50 g. butter	¼ cup butter
2 oz./50 g. chocolate	2 oz. chocolate
4 oz./100 g. icing sugar	1 cup sifted confectioners' sugar
4 oz./100 g. stale cake crumbs	2 cups stale cake crumbs
1 oz./25 g. desiccated coconut	⅓ cup shredded coconut
2 oz./50 g. ground almonds	½ cup ground almonds
2 tablespoons rum	3 tablespoons rum
coating	**coating**
sieved apricot jam	sieved apricot jam
chocolate vermicelli	chocolate vermicelli

Melt the butter in a bowl over hot water then add the chocolate. Sieve the icing sugar into a bowl and mix with the crumbs, coconut and ground almonds. Pour the chocolate mixture over the crumbs, add the rum and mix well. Shape into small balls, dip in sieved warmed apricot jam and roll in chocolate vermicelli.

Australian shortcake

Preparation time 15 minutes
Cooking time 45–50 minutes

IMPERIAL/METRIC	AMERICAN
6 oz./175 g. butter	¾ cup butter
3 oz./75 g. soft brown sugar	6 tablespoons soft brown sugar
3 oz./75 g. castor sugar	6 tablespoons sugar
2 eggs	2 eggs
½ teaspoon vanilla essence	½ teaspoon vanilla extract
8 oz./225 g. plain flour	2 cups all-purpose flour
1 oz./25 g. desiccated coconut	⅓ cup shredded coconut
filling	**filling**
2 oz./50 g. butter	¼ cup butter
3 oz./75 g. soft brown sugar	6 tablespoons soft brown sugar
3 oz./75 g. currants	½ cup currants
1 oz./25 g. desiccated coconut	⅓ cup shredded coconut
1 oz./25 g. mixed peel	3 tablespoons mixed peel
1 oz./25 g. glacé cherries, chopped	3 tablespoons chopped candied cherries
3 teaspoons cinnamon	3 teaspoons cinnamon
1 teaspoon brandy or sherry	1 teaspoon brandy or sherry
to decorate	**to decorate**
4 oz./100 g. icing sugar, sieved	1 cup sifted confectioners' sugar
1½ tablespoons water	2 tablespoons water
glacé cherries	candied cherries
angelica	candied angelica

Cream together the butter and sugar until light and fluffy. Add the eggs, beating in one at a time, then add the vanilla essence. Fold in the flour and coconut.

Melt the butter and sugar for the filling in a pan, remove from the heat and add the remaining ingredients. Spread half the shortcake mixture on the bottom of a well greased 7-inch (18-cm.) cake tin, cover with the filling and top with the remaining shortcake mixture. Bake in a moderate oven (350°F., 180°C., Gas Mark 4) for 45–50 minutes. When cooled, cover the top with glacé icing, made by mixing the icing sugar and water, and allow it to run down the sides. Decorate with glacé cherries and angelica.

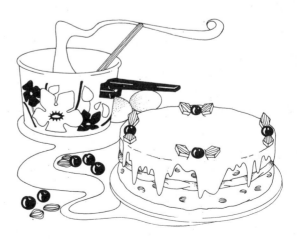

Chocolate mint cakes

Preparation time 20 minutes
Cooking time 10–12 minutes
Makes 18

IMPERIAL/METRIC	AMERICAN
4 oz./100 g. plain chocolate	4 squares (4 oz.) semi-sweet chocolate
3 oz./75 g. butter	6 tablespoons butter
2 oz./50 g. castor sugar	¼ cup sugar
3 eggs	3 eggs
3 oz./75 g. plain flour	¾ cup all-purpose flour
½ teaspoon baking powder	½ teaspoon baking powder
icing	**icing**
8 oz./225 g. icing sugar	2 cups sifted confectioners' sugar
2 tablespoons water	3 tablespoons water
3 drops peppermint essence	3 drops peppermint extract
2–3 drops green food colouring	2–3 drops green food coloring
to decorate	**to decorate**
chocolate peppermints	chocolate-covered peppermint candies

Prepare 18 well greased patty tins or paper cake cases. Melt the chocolate in a small bowl over hot water. Cream the butter and sugar together until light and fluffy. Separate the eggs and beat the yolks into the melted chocolate. Add this to the creamed mixture, beating well. Whisk the egg whites and, using a metal spoon, fold into the mixture alternating with the sieved flour and baking powder. Half fill the prepared tins and bake in a moderately hot oven (375°F., 190°C., Gas Mark 5) for about 10–12 minutes. Remove from the tins and cool on a wire tray.

To make the icing, sieve the icing sugar and add the water very gradually beating well all the time. Add the peppermint essence and green colouring from a skewer, after the first tablespoon of water. The icing is ready to use when it coats the back of a wooden spoon. Pour a spoonful of icing on to each cake and spread over the top. Top with a halved chocolate peppermint cream.

Apricot layer desserts

ILLUSTRATED IN COLOUR ON PAGE 39
Preparation time 10 minutes
Cooking time about 10 minutes
Serves 4–6

IMPERIAL/METRIC	AMERICAN
3 oz./75 g. butter	6 tablespoons butter
8 oz./225 g. soft brown breadcrumbs	4 cups soft brown bread crumbs
2 oz./50 g. demerara sugar	¼ cup brown sugar
1 (1 lb. 13-oz./800-g.) can apricot halves	1 (1 lb. 13-oz.) can apricot halves
½ oz./15 g. arrowroot	2 tablespoons arrowroot flour
to decorate	**to decorate**
¼ pint/1½ dl. double cream, whipped	⅔ cup whipping cream
glacé cherries	candied cherries

Melt the butter over a gentle heat and use to fry the breadcrumbs quickly until crisp and golden. Stir in the sugar. Drain the apricots and make up the syrup with water, if necessary, to make ½ pint (3 dl., 1¼ cups). Blend together the measured syrup and arrowroot and heat gently, stirring constantly, until thickened and clear. Place layers of buttered crumbs, apricot halves and thickened syrup in sundae glasses, finishing with apricots and syrup. Pipe a rosette of whipped cream on top of each dessert and decorate each with a glacé cherry.

Butterscotch cake

Preparation time 15 minutes
Cooking time 15–20 minutes

IMPERIAL/METRIC	AMERICAN
5 oz./150 g. plain flour	1¼ cups all-purpose flour
2 teaspoons baking powder	2 teaspoons baking powder
5 oz./150 g. soft brown sugar	⅔ cup soft brown sugar
5 tablespoons corn oil	6 tablespoons corn oil
5 tablespoons milk	6 tablespoons milk
1 tablespoon coffee essence	1 tablespoon coffee extract
2 eggs, separated	2 eggs, separated
icing	**icing**
8 oz./225 g. icing sugar	1¾ cups sifted confectioners' sugar
3 oz./75 g. margarine or butter	6 tablespoons margarine or butter
1 tablespoon coffee essence	1 tablespoon coffee extract
1 tablespoon milk	1 tablespoon milk

Sieve the flour and baking powder into a bowl. Stir in the sugar. Blend the oil, milk and coffee essence. Beat in the egg yolks and add all the liquid to the dry ingredients. Beat well until a smooth batter is formed. Whisk the egg whites until stiff and fold into the mixture. Grease and line 2 (7-inch/18-cm.) sandwich tins. Divide the mixture between the tins. Bake in a preheated moderately hot oven (400°F., 200°C., Gas Mark 6) for 15–20 minutes. Turn out and cool on a wire tray.

To make the icing, place all the ingredients together in a mixing bowl and beat until smooth. Sandwich the cakes together with a third of the icing and spread the remainder on top. Decorate with grated chocolate, if liked.

Cheese tarts

Preparation time 20 minutes
Cooking time 30 minutes
Makes 24

IMPERIAL/METRIC	AMERICAN
4 oz./100 g. shortcrust pastry using 4 oz./100 g. plain flour	basic pie dough using 1 cup all-purpose flour etc.
filling	**filling**
2 eggs	2 eggs
2 oz./50 g. castor sugar	¼ cup castor sugar
1 oz./25 g. ground almonds	¼ cup ground almonds
2 oz./50 g. cheese, grated	½ cup grated cheese
1 oz./25 g. butter, melted	2 tablespoons melted butter
1 oz./25 g. self-raising flour	¼ cup all-purpose flour sifted with ½ teaspoon baking powder
2 tablespoons raspberry jam	3 tablespoons raspberry jam

Roll out the shortcrust pastry thinly on a lightly floured board and cut into 3-inch (7·5-cm.) circles with a pastry cutter. Line two patty trays with the pastry circles and prick the bases with a fork.

Whisk the egg yolks with the sugar until the mixture is light and fluffy. Fold in the ground almonds and grated cheese, then add the melted butter and fold in the sifted flour and whisked egg whites. Put a spot of jam on the bottom of each pastry case and a spoonful of mixture on top. Bake in a moderate oven (350°F., 180°C., Gas Mark 4) for 30 minutes. Cool on a wire tray.

Double-quick ideas for extra busy days

Does your heart sink when the telephone goes, and the question is – can I bring someone home for a meal? Maybe the washing machine is out of order, with a stack of grubby laundry for the local football team waiting; or you've just started turning out the cupboard under the stairs! Finding time to cook extra dainties seems impossible, and you had been counting on whipping up a quick meal in 10 minutes. All is not lost. Salads take little time to prepare. My favourite is Chef's salad; you may prefer Anchovied egg salad, put the eggs on to hard boil in the time it takes to prepare the rest of the meal and set the table. Eggs are superb when time is short – the most delicious omelette in the world only requires 4 minutes to cook. Stuffed omelettes can be adventurous in taste contrast; chopped olives, mushrooms, pimento, cooked new potatoes, green peas, chopped tomato, crisp bacon bits, chopped smoked sausage – it's easier to decide what you *can't* put in an omelette than what you can! An open omelette covered with bacon slices and cooked vegetables is a fine filler.

Sausages, too, are versatile. Split and stuffed with a mustardy mixture, rolled in processed cheese slices and grilled, or in pastry and baked. They also combine with grilled pineapple rings, or mashed potato and a slither of cooked onion blended with baked beans.

How about fried sandwiches, soaked in egg and milk, put together with cheese, sardines, tuna or salmon, and topped with canned fruit then fried golden brown? Or club sandwiches, three layers of toast, still warm and pressed together with a salad layer and a cooked chicken mayonnaise layer. For guests, top with a saucy cocktail stick, skewering together gherkins, tiny tomatoes,

Tijuana pie (page 54), kidneys in rice ring (page 57) and goujons of plaice (page 52) with zippy orange sauce (page 53).

cheese squares, pineapple cubes, olives. Coleslaw goes well with either of these. Just grated white cabbage, half the quantity of carrot and half again of apple, tossed together with French dressing or mayonnaise diluted with cream or natural yogurt. A basic French dressing is quickly made by putting a teaspoon of salt and a quarter teaspoon each of white pepper and sugar in a wide-necked jar. Add 4 tablespoons wine vinegar and 6 tablespoons corn or olive oil. Screw on the lid and shake vigorously to emulsify.

For a make-believe continental jaunt, frankfurters with sauerkraut soon becomes familiar and pleasing. I always have a can of frankfurters and another of sauerkraut, ready for emergencies. Both need gently heating, not cooking, especially since the frankfurters resent it and burst. Add caraway seeds to the sauerkraut, mild German mustard to the frankfurters, and top with gherkin fans. Small potatoes, even if they are not new ones, go well with this. If you just have time to scrub but not peel them, wash well and boil in the skins. Glaze the skins with melted butter and then titivate them with chopped parsley.

Cheese, of course, cooks quickly and takes other forms, whether melted in beer for rarebits or stirred into a seasoned white sauce and used to blanket cooked cauliflower or Jerusalem artichokes. Or make the sauce really thick, cool and roll into cork shapes to make croquettes. Coated in flour, then in egg and then toasted crumbs – they fry in a few minutes to a rich brown colour. Croquettes are a treat with any cold meat, especially ham. Ham rolls with a cream cottage cheese filling are good; just mash the cottage cheese with cream, mustard, chopped herbs, or crushed canned pineapple or peaches.

51

Anchovied egg salad

Preparation time 20 minutes
Serves 4

IMPERIAL/METRIC	AMERICAN
8 oz./225 g. tomatoes	½ lb. tomatoes
4 hard-boiled eggs	4 hard-cooked eggs
1 (7-oz./200-g.) can anchovy fillets	1 (7-oz.) can anchovy fillets
1 tablespoon chopped salted peanuts	1 tablespoon chopped salted peanuts
½ cucumber, sliced	½ cucumber, sliced
2 tablespoons mayonnaise	3 tablespoons mayonnaise
1 tablespoon single cream	1 tablespoon coffee cream
paprika pepper	paprika pepper
parsley sprigs	parsley sprigs

Using a sharp pointed knife, 'Vandyke' the tomatoes round the circumference and pull apart. Slice the eggs in half lengthways and scoop out the yolks. Reserve a few anchovy fillets for the garnish and chop the rest with their oil. Add the egg yolks and mash well together. Stir in the chopped peanuts and use this mixture to fill the egg white halves.

Place a bed of cucumber slices on a serving dish and place the filled egg halves, rounded side up, on this with the tomato halves. Thin the mayonnaise, if necessary, with the cream and spoon a little over each egg half. Decorate with the reserved anchovy fillets and dust with paprika pepper. Place a tiny parsley sprig in each tomato 'cup'.

Goujons of plaice

ILLUSTRATED IN COLOUR ON PAGE 50
Preparation time 10 minutes
Cooking time about 6 minutes
Serves 4

IMPERIAL/METRIC	AMERICAN
1 (13-oz./375-g.) packet frozen plaice fillets, defrosted	1 (13-oz.) package frozen sole fillets, defrosted
salt and freshly ground black pepper	salt and freshly ground black pepper
little lemon juice	little lemon juice
2 eggs, beaten	2 eggs, beaten
4–6 oz./100–175 g. fine dry white breadcrumbs	1–2 cups fine dry white bread crumbs
oil for frying	oil for frying
2 lemons	2 lemons
watercress sprigs	watercress sprigs

Separate the fillets and cut each into thin strips. Season with salt and pepper and a sprinkling of lemon juice. Coat the fish strips with beaten egg and then with breadcrumbs. Shallow fry the goujons in hot oil for about 6 minutes altogether, turning frequently, until golden brown on all sides. Or fry in hot deep oil for 4–5 minutes. Drain the fish well and serve hot or cold with lemon wedges and garnished with watercress sprigs. Hand Zippy orange sauce (see page opposite) separately.

Nutty ham rolls

Preparation time 15 minutes
Serves 4

IMPERIAL/METRIC	AMERICAN
1 (11-oz./310-g.) can sweet corn	1 (11-oz.) can corn kernels
6 oz./175 g. cream cheese	¾ cup cream cheese
4 oz./100 g. Lancashire cheese, crumbled	1 cup crumbled cheese
2 sticks celery, chopped	2 stalks celery, chopped
2 oz./50 g. walnuts, chopped	½ cup chopped walnuts
2 red-skinned eating apples	2 red-skinned eating apples
salt and pepper to taste	salt and pepper to taste
8 thin slices cooked ham	8 thin slices cooked cured ham
lemon juice	lemon juice
to garnish	**to garnish**
watercress	watercress

Drain the sweetcorn and place on a serving dish. Beat 2 tablespoons of liquid from the sweet corn can into the cream cheese and fold in the crumbled Lancashire cheese, celery and walnuts. Core and dice one apple, stir into the cheese mixture and season well. Divide the filling between the slices of ham and roll up neatly. Place the rolls on the bed of sweet corn. Core the remaining apple and cut it into slices. Sprinkle the apple slices with lemon juice and use to garnish with the watercress.

Chef's salad

Preparation time 15–20 minutes
Serves 4

IMPERIAL/METRIC	AMERICAN
1 clove garlic	1 clove garlic
1 medium lettuce	1 medium lettuce
4 oz./100 g. cooked ham	¼ lb. cooked cured ham
4 oz./100 g. Cheddar cheese, grated	1 cup grated Cheddar cheese
2 hard-boiled eggs, sliced	2 hard-cooked eggs, sliced
2 tomatoes, sliced	2 tomatoes, sliced
4 tablespoons French dressing (see page 51)	⅓ cup French dressing (see page 51)
salt and freshly ground pepper	salt and freshly ground pepper
to garnish	**to garnish**
fried bread croûtons	fried bread croûtons

Rub the inside of a salad bowl with the cut clove of garlic. Tear the lettuce into 2-inch (5-cm.) widths. Cut the ham in narrow strips. Lightly toss the lettuce, ham, cheese, eggs and tomatoes with the dressing and seasoning. Serve immediately garnished with croûtons.

Zippy orange sauce

Preparation time 10 minutes
Cooking time 10 minutes
Serves 4

IMPERIAL/METRIC	AMERICAN
1 orange, peeled	1 orange, peeled
½ (6-fl. oz./¼-litre) can frozen orange concentrate	½ (6-fl. oz.) can frozen orange concentrate
1 tablespoon lemon juice	1 tablespoon lemon juice
salt and pepper to taste	salt and pepper to taste
½ teaspoon dry mustard	½ teaspoon dry mustard
1 teaspoon arrowroot	1 teaspoon arrowroot flour

Divide the orange into segments over a measuring jug, removing all pith and skin. Reserve the segments. Add the frozen orange concentrate to the juice and make up to ½ pint (3 dl., 1¼ cups) with cold water. Place in a saucepan with the lemon juice, seasoning and mustard and bring to the boil, stirring. Moisten the arrowroot with 2 tablespoons water and add to the pan, stirring constantly, until the sauce thickens and is almost clear. Remove from the heat and stir in the orange segments. Taste and adjust seasoning. Reheat to boiling point and simmer for 1 minute.

Tijuana pie

ILLUSTRATED IN COLOUR ON PAGE 50
Preparation time 20 minutes
Cooking time 35 minutes
Serves 6

IMPERIAL/METRIC	AMERICAN
1 (13-oz./375-g.) packet frozen shortcrust pastry, defrosted	1 (13-oz.) package frozen basic pie dough, defrosted
1 small green pepper	1 small green sweet pepper
2 tablespoons oil	3 tablespoons oil
1 medium onion, chopped	1 medium onion, chopped
1 lb./450 g. minced beef	1 lb. ground beef
1 teaspoon salt	1 teaspoon salt
$\frac{1}{4}$ teaspoon freshly ground black pepper	$\frac{1}{4}$ teaspoon freshly ground black pepper
$\frac{1}{2}$–1 tablespoon chilli powder	$\frac{1}{2}$–1 tablespoon chili powder
1 teaspoon cornflour	1 teaspoon cornstarch
8 fl. oz./2$\frac{1}{4}$ dl. tomato juice	scant 1 cup tomato juice
2 oz./50 g. stuffed green olives, sliced	$\frac{1}{2}$ cup sliced stuffed green olives

Roll out two-thirds of the pastry and use to line an 8–9-inch (20–23-cm.) flan ring standing on a greased baking sheet.

Deseed and chop the green pepper. Heat the oil and use to fry the onion and green pepper together for 5 minutes. Add the beef and cook quickly until browned, stirring frequently. Add the seasonings, cornflour and tomato juice mixed, then stir well. Simmer uncovered for 15 minutes. Cool. Stir in the olives and spoon the filling into the pastry case. Roll out the remaining pastry and cut into thin strips. Arrange over the meat filling in a lattice pattern. Bake in a moderately hot oven (400°F., 200°C., Gas Mark 6) for 35 minutes or until the pastry is well browned.

Pickled onion omelette

Preparation time 20 minutes
Cooking time 10 minutes
Serves 4

IMPERIAL/METRIC	AMERICAN
2 pickled onions	2 pickled onions
1 tomato, peeled	1 tomato, peeled
1 oz./25 g. small pasta shapes	$\frac{1}{4}$ cup small pasta shapes
4 rashers streaky bacon	4 bacon slices
1 oz./25 g. butter	2 tablespoons butter
4 eggs	4 eggs
1 tablespoon chopped fresh mixed herbs	1 tablespoon chopped fresh mixed herbs
salt and pepper to taste	salt and pepper to taste
4 tablespoons cooked peas	$\frac{1}{3}$ cup cooked peas

Finely chop the onions and roughly chop the tomato. Cook the pasta shapes in plenty of boiling, salted water until tender. Drain. Grill the bacon until crisp. Melt the butter in a heavy-based frying pan and use to fry the onion until soft but not coloured. Whisk together the eggs, 2 tablespoons cold water, herbs and seasoning, and pour over the cooked onion. Stir in the peas, tomato and cooked pasta. Cook gently, stirring the centre and loosening the edges until set. Place under a hot grill until the top is a light golden colour. Place the crisp bacon round the outside of the pan and serve cut into wedges.

Salmon and asparagus flan

Preparation time 15 minutes
Cooking time 30 minutes
Serves 4

IMPERIAL/METRIC	AMERICAN
8 oz./225 g. frozen shortcrust pastry, defrosted	½ lb. frozen basic pie dough, defrosted
¼ pint/1½ dl. milk	⅔ cup milk
1 (15-oz./425-g.) can green asparagus spears	1 (15-oz.) can green asparagus spears
1 oz./25 g. butter or margarine	2 tablespoons butter or margarine
1 oz./25 g. flour	¼ cup all-purpose flour
salt and pepper to taste	salt and pepper to taste
1 (7½-oz./215-g.) can pink salmon, drained	1 (7½-oz.) can pink salmon, drained
2 oz./50 g. Gouda cheese, grated	½ cup grated Gouda cheese

Roll out the pastry thinly and use to line an 8-inch (20-cm.) flan ring standing on a baking sheet. Bake blind in a moderately hot oven (375°F., 190°C., Gas Mark 5) for 25 minutes. (To save time, bake the flan case in advance or use a baked pastry flan case from the freezer. Defrost in the oven while it heats up.)

Make the milk up to ½ pint (3 dl., 1¼ cups) with the liquid from the can of asparagus. Melt the butter, stir in the flour and cook for 2 minutes. Gradually add the flavoured milk and bring to the boil, stirring constantly, until the sauce is smooth and thick. Season to taste and stir in the flaked salmon. Cool slightly and pour into the baked flan case. Arrange the asparagus spears pointing out from the centre of the flan and sprinkle with cheese. Raise the oven heat to moderately hot (400°F., 200°C., Gas Mark 6) and return the flan to the oven for a further 5 minutes, until the cheese has melted.

Creamy ham towers

Preparation time 15 minutes
Cooking time 15 minutes
Serves 6

IMPERIAL/METRIC	AMERICAN
6 vol-au-vent cases, baked	6 vol-au-vent cases, baked
1 (10-oz./280-g.) can condensed asparagus soup	1 (10-oz.) can condensed asparagus soup
8 oz./225 g. cooked ham, diced	1 cup diced cooked cured ham
1 tablespoon chopped pimento	1 tablespoon chopped pimiento
1 tablespoon chopped parsley	1 tablespoon chopped parsley
scant ¼ pint/1½ dl. soured cream or double cream and 1 teaspoon lemon juice	scant ⅔ cup sour cream or whipping cream and 1 teaspoon lemon juice
few green or black olives, sliced	few green or ripe olives, sliced

Place the vol-au-vent cases in a hot oven (425°F., 220°C., Gas Mark 7) for 5 minutes to crisp. Keep warm while preparing the filling. Heat the soup to boiling point and stir in the ham, pimento and parsley. Cook over low heat until thoroughly heated and stir in the soured cream. Heat until piping hot but do not allow to boil. Spoon into the hot vol-au-vent cases and serve garnished with sliced olives.

Quick pork grill

Preparation time 10 minutes
Cooking time about 30 minutes
Serves 4

IMPERIAL/METRIC	AMERICAN
4 thin pork chops	4 thin pork chops
1 tablespoon oil	1 tablespoon oil
salt and pepper	salt and pepper
1 lb./450 g. frozen broccoli	1 lb. frozen broccoli
1 lb./450 g. frozen potato chips	1 lb. frozen French fries
oil for frying	oil for frying
1 orange	1 orange
1 oz./25 g. blanched almonds	¼ cup blanched almonds
1 oz./25 g. butter	2 tablespoons butter
2 teaspoons honey	2 teaspoons honey

Brush the chops lightly with oil and sprinkle with salt and pepper. Grill on both sides until brown and crisp. Meanwhile, cook the broccoli and fry the chips in hot oil. Grate the zest from half the orange and squeeze all the juice. Cut the almonds into slivers. Melt the butter and toss the nuts in it until pale golden then sprinkle with salt and pepper and add the orange zest, juice and honey to the pan. Stir briskly over the heat for 1 minute. Arrange the chops, chips and some broccoli on a hot serving dish and spoon the sauce over the chops. Serve the remaining broccoli separately.

Chilli cheese log

Preparation time 15 minutes plus chilling time

IMPERIAL/METRIC	AMERICAN
4 oz./100 g. cream cheese	½ cup cream cheese
8 oz./225 g. Cheddar cheese, grated	2 cups grated Cheddar cheese
1½ teaspoons lemon juice	1½ teaspoons lemon juice
½ teaspoon chilli powder	½ teaspoon chili powder
½ teaspoon paprika pepper	¼ teaspoon paprika pepper
2 oz./50 g. pecan or similar nuts	½ cup pecan or similar nuts

Let the cheese stand at room temperature to soften. Beat together the cream cheese, Cheddar cheese, lemon juice, chilli powder and paprika pepper. Shape in a roll about 1½ inches (3·5 cm.) in diameter. Finely chop the pecan nuts and roll the cheese shape in these to coat. Chill until ready to serve. Serve with lightly buttered rusks or savoury biscuits.

Creamy Camembert toasts

Preparation time 10 minutes plus 12 hours marinating time
Serves 4

IMPERIAL/METRIC	AMERICAN
1 half box very ripe Camembert	1 half box very ripe Camembert
dry white wine	dry white wine
2 oz./50 g. unsalted butter, softened	¼ cup softened sweet butter
4 peach halves, peeled	4 peach halves, peeled

Use Camembert which is soft and runny to make a tasty French savoury. Place it in a deep bowl, peeled or unpeeled, and pour over enough wine to barely cover. Leave for at least 12 hours. Add the softened butter and work in well to form a smooth paste.

Place fresh or canned peach halves, cut side down, on lightly buttered toast. Cover with the mixture and place under a hot grill until the cheese begins to bubble.

Kidneys in rice ring

ILLUSTRATED IN COLOUR ON PAGE 50
Preparation time 15 minutes
Cooking time 20 minutes
Serves 4

IMPERIAL/METRIC	AMERICAN
3 packets frozen braised kidneys in gravy	3 packages frozen braised kidneys in gravy
2 packets frozen savoury vegetable rice (mushrooms and peas)	2 packages frozen savory vegetable rice (mushrooms and peas)
6 tablespoons red wine	½ cup red wine

Cook the kidneys and rice as directed on the packets. Meanwhile, place the wine in a saucepan and boil over high heat, until reduced by half. Lightly oil a ring mould. Press the cooked rice into the mould and turn out on to a hot serving dish. Pour the cooked kidneys out of the packets into the reduced wine and stir thoroughly. Reheat to boiling point then spoon the kidney mixture carefully into the rice ring.

Turkey divan

Preparation time 15 minutes
Cooking time about 15 minutes
Serves 3

IMPERIAL/METRIC	AMERICAN
1 (10-oz./275-g.) can condensed cream of chicken soup	1 (10-oz.) can condensed cream of chicken soup
4 fl. oz./1¼ dl. milk	scant ⅔ cup milk
pinch ground mace	pinch ground mace
1 tablespoon sherry	1 tablespoon sherry
10 oz./275 g. frozen broccoli	10 oz. frozen broccoli
6 slices turkey	6 slices turkey
3 oz./75 g. Cheddar cheese, grated	¾ cup grated Cheddar cheese

Mix together the soup, milk, mace and sherry in a saucepan. Bring slowly to the boil, stirring frequently. Cook the broccoli and drain. Arrange the broccoli in a shallow ovenproof casserole and cover with the turkey slices. Pour the soup mixture over and sprinkle with grated cheese. Place under a medium hot grill until the cheese has melted and the mixture is heated through.

Golden summer savoury

Preparation time 10 minutes
Cooking time 10 minutes
Serves 4

IMPERIAL/METRIC	AMERICAN
1 bunch spring onions	1 bunch scallions
1 (8-oz./225-g.) can sweetcorn	1 (8-oz.) can corn kernels
12 oz./350 g. canned ham	¾ lb. canned cured ham
1 oz./25 g. butter	2 tablespoons butter
½ teaspoon turmeric	½ teaspoon turmeric
salt and pepper	salt and pepper
8 oz./225 g. frozen petits pois	½ lb. frozen petits pois
2 slices white bread, toasted	2 slices white bread, toasted

Trim the spring onions, reserving a few for the garnish, and finely chop the rest. Drain the corn and dice the ham. Melt the butter and use to fry the ham gently until browned on all sides. Stir in the corn and onion. Season to taste with the turmeric, salt and pepper.

Meanwhile, cook the petits pois, drain and place in the base of a warm serving dish. Cover with the ham and corn mixture. Trim the crusts from the hot toast and cut the toast into neat triangles. Use these to garnish and place the reserved spring onions on top.

Californian burgers

Preparation time 15 minutes
Cooking time 20 minutes
Serves 4

IMPERIAL/METRIC	AMERICAN
2 oz./50 g. tender prunes	$\frac{1}{3}$ cup tender prunes
1 dessert apple	1 dessert apple
1 soft roll, soaked	1 soft roll, soaked
1 lb./450 g. minced beef	1 lb. ground beef
1 egg, beaten	1 egg, beaten
salt and pepper to taste	salt and pepper to taste
4 tablespoons seasoned flour	$\frac{1}{3}$ cup seasoned flour
2 oz./50 g. lard or dripping	$\frac{1}{4}$ cup lard or drippings
4 oz./100 g. mushrooms	1 cup mushrooms
4 large tomatoes, halved	4 large tomatoes, halved

Pour boiling water over the prunes and allow to stand for a few minutes, until they can be halved and the stones removed. Chop finely. Core and chop the apple without peeling. Squeeze out the soaked bread roll and mix with the beef, apple, prunes and beaten egg. Season generously with salt and pepper and add a little water from soaking the prunes if necessary, to make the mixture manageable. Shape into 8 small cakes and turn in seasoned flour.

Melt half the lard and use to fry the burgers on each side for about 5 minutes, until golden brown. Keep hot. Melt the remaining lard in a separate pan and use to cook the mushrooms and tomato halves. Serve with crisply fried chips or creamy mashed potato, garnishing each portion with 2 tomato halves and a few mushrooms.

Sausage bubble and squeak

Preparation time 10 minutes
Cooking time 25 minutes
Serves 4–6

IMPERIAL/METRIC	AMERICAN
$\frac{1}{2}$ oz./15 g. butter	1 tablespoon butter
1 lb./450 g. sausages	1 lb. sausages
4 oz./100 g. bacon, chopped	$\frac{1}{4}$ lb. bacon slices or Canadian bacon, chopped
1–2 onions, sliced	1–2 onions, sliced
1 lb./450 g. potatoes, cooked and diced	1 lb. potatoes, cooked and diced
1 lb./450 g. Brussels sprouts, cooked	1 lb. Brussels sprouts, cooked
salt and freshly ground pepper	salt and freshly ground pepper

Melt the butter and use to fry the sausages until golden brown all over. Remove from the pan and keep hot. Add the bacon and onion to the remaining fat and fry gently until softened. Mix in the diced potato and whole sprouts and continue frying until heated through, stirring frequently. Remove any excess fat. Season to taste with salt and freshly ground pepper. Cut the sausages into chunks, add to the pan and mix well. Serve piping hot.

Pasta snack

Preparation time 10 minutes
Cooking time about 30 minutes
Serves 4–6

IMPERIAL/METRIC	AMERICAN
8 oz./225 g. spaghetti	½ lb. spaghetti
2 oz./50 g. butter	¼ cup butter
1 tablespoon chopped parsley	1 tablespoon chopped parsley
freshly ground black pepper	freshly ground black pepper
12–16 oz./350–450 g. smoked haddock or cod fillet	¾–1 lb. smoked haddock or cod fillet
lemon juice to taste	lemon juice to taste
3 eggs, beaten	3 eggs, beaten

Cook the spaghetti in 4 pints (2¼ litres, 10 cups) of well-salted boiling water for 14 minutes or until just tender. Drain in a colander, then return to the hot pan with the butter and parsley, seasoning well with black pepper.

Meanwhile, poach the smoked fish for 12–15 minutes in boiling water, then drain and flake. Mix the fish into the spaghetti and season to taste with lemon juice.

Turn the spaghetti and fish into a hot serving dish and stir in the beaten eggs. When thoroughly mixed, serve immediately with wooden pasta forks or salad servers.

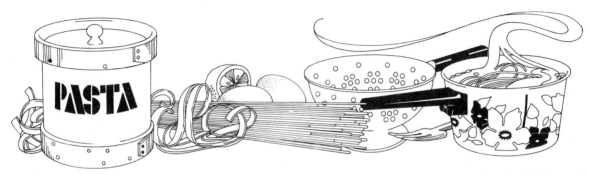

Ham steak fry

Preparation time 10 minutes
Cooking time 15 minutes
Serves 4

IMPERIAL/METRIC	AMERICAN
4 medium thick sweetcure ham steaks	4 medium thick cured ham slices
1 egg	1 egg
2 tablespoons milk	3 tablespoons milk
1 packet lemon and thyme stuffing	1 package lemon and thyme or other savory stuffing mix
1 celery heart, trimmed	1 celery heart, trimmed
2 oz./50 g. butter	¼ cup butter
salt and pepper to taste	salt and pepper to taste
2 tablespoons oil	3 tablespoons oil
1 lb./450 g. broad or runner beans, cooked	1 lb. lima or green beans, cooked
1 tablespoon chopped parsley	1 tablespoon chopped parsley

Cut each slice of ham in half to make two half-moon shapes. Lightly beat the egg with the milk and use to coat the ham. Dip in the dry stuffing mixture. Dice the celery and parboil in boiling, salted water. Drain well and toss in half the butter over high heat until golden brown. Drain well, season with salt and pepper and keep hot. Meanwhile, heat the remaining butter and the oil and use to fry the coated ham steaks until crisp and golden brown on both sides. Arrange on a warm serving dish and sprinkle the diced celery over. Pile the cooked beans in the centre of the dish and top with chopped parsley.

Fried sandwiches

Preparation time 10 minutes
Cooking time about 8 minutes per sandwich
Serves 4

IMPERIAL/METRIC	AMERICAN
2 eggs	2 eggs
4 tablespoons milk	⅓ cup milk
salt and pepper to taste	salt and pepper to taste
1 (4½-oz./125-g.) can sardines in oil	1 (4½-oz.) can sardines in oil
2 oz./50 g. butter	¼ cup butter
8 slices white bread, trimmed	8 slices white bread, trimmed
2 oz./50 g. Gouda cheese, grated	½ cup grated Gouda cheese
2 tablespoons oil	3 tablespoons oil
watercress sprigs	watercress sprigs

Beat together the eggs and milk, season to taste and pour into a shallow dish. Drain the sardines and mix the sardine oil with half the butter and use to spread the bread slices thinly on one side. Mash the sardines, spread on half the bread slices on one side only and top this with grated cheese. Place the remaining bread slices, buttered side down, on top and press together firmly. Dip the sandwiches quickly in the egg mixture on both sides, turning with food tongs or a fish slice.

Heat together the remaining butter and the oil and use to fry the sandwiches on both sides until golden brown. Place on a hot serving platter and garnish with sprigs of watercress.

Layered pineapple beanfeast

Preparation time 5 minutes
Cooking time 15 minutes
Serves 4

IMPERIAL/METRIC	AMERICAN
1 tablespoon oil	1 tablespoon oil
3 oz./75 g. butter	6 tablespoons butter
4 slices bread, trimmed	4 slices bread, trimmed
4 pineapple rings	4 pineapple rings
8 slices luncheon meat	8 slices luncheon meat
1 (8-oz./225-g.) can baked beans	1 (8-oz.) can baked beans
1 tablespoon sweet brown chutney, chopped	1 tablespoon sweet brown chutney or relish, chopped

Heat together the oil and 1 oz. (25 g., 2 tablespoons) of the butter and use to fry the bread slices on both sides until golden brown. Drain and pat the pineapple rings dry with absorbent kitchen paper. Add the remaining butter to the pan and use to fry the pineapple rings lightly on both sides. Remove the pineapple and fry the luncheon meat slices in the same way.

Meanwhile heat the baked beans. Spread a layer of beans on each piece of fried bread and top with 2 slices of fried luncheon meat, then the pineapple rings. Place a little sweet brown chutney in the centre of each pineapple ring.

Beef sausage bake

Preparation time 15 minutes
Cooking time 35 minutes in total
Serves 4

IMPERIAL/METRIC	AMERICAN
2 oz./50 g. butter	¼ cup butter
1 lb./450 g. beef sausages	1 lb. beef sausages
1–2 large onions, sliced	1–2 large onions, sliced
1½ lb./700 g. mashed potato	3 cups mashed potato
1 egg, beaten	1 egg, beaten
salt and pepper to taste	salt and pepper to taste
1–2 oz./25–50 g. cheese, grated	¼–½ cup grated cheese

Melt half the butter and use to fry the sausages until golden brown all over, then remove from the pan. Add the sliced onion and fry until softened and just turning colour. Put the mashed potato in a large bowl and mix in the onion with the butter. Stir in the beaten egg and season to taste. Turn the potato mixture into a shallow ovenproof dish, level it off and scatter with grated cheese. Press in the sausages and dot the potato with remaining butter. Bake in a moderately hot oven (400°F., 200°C., Gas Mark 6) for 20 minutes until the potato has risen and is golden brown.

Savoury stuffed peaches

Preparation time 10 minutes
Serves 6

IMPERIAL/METRIC	AMERICAN
1 (16-oz./450-g.) can peach halves	1 (16-oz.) can peach halves
1 (3¾-oz./110-g.) can tuna, drained	1 (3¾-oz.) can tuna, drained
1 (¼-pint/1½-dl.) carton soured cream	1 (⅔-cup) carton sour cream
1 oz./25 g. small gherkins, chopped	2 tablespoons chopped small dill pickles
1 oz./25 g. stuffed olives, sliced	2 tablespoons sliced stuffed olives
1 teaspoon chopped chives	1 teaspoon chopped chives
salt and pepper to taste	salt and pepper to taste
few lettuce leaves	few lettuce leaves
to garnish	**to garnish**
parsley sprigs	parsley sprigs

Drain the peaches well and place cut side down on absorbent kitchen paper. To make the filling, first flake the tuna. Beat the soured cream until smooth and fold in the tuna, gherkins, olives and chives.

Season to taste and divide between the peach 'cups', moulding up well in the centre.

Top each with a parsley sprig and arrange on a bed of lettuce leaves.

Inishmaan fish

Preparation time 10–15 minutes
Cooking time about 10 minutes
Serves 4

IMPERIAL/METRIC	AMERICAN
3 large scallops or 8 oz./225 g. smaller ones	3 large scallops or ½ lb. smaller ones
8 oz./225 g. soft cod or herring roes	½ lb. soft cod or herring roes
4 oz./100 g. butter	½ cup butter
8 oz./225 g. mussels, cooked	½ lb. mussels, cooked
8 oz./225 g. cockles, cooked	½ lb. cockles or small clams, cooked
8 oz./225 g. Dublin Bay prawns, cooked	½ lb. jumbo-sized shrimp, cooked
freshly ground pepper	freshly ground pepper
3 tablespoons lemon juice	¼ cup lemon juice
lemon butter	**lemon butter**
4 oz./100 g. butter	½ cup butter
1 lemon	1 lemon
to garnish	**to garnish**
chopped parsley	chopped parsley

First make the lemon butter. Cream the butter and gradually work in the finely grated rind of the lemon and 2 tablespoons juice. Place in a small serving dish, rough up the top with the blade of a knife and chill before serving.

Slice the scallops and roes. Melt the butter in a wide pan, put in the scallops and roes. Cook for about 5 minutes, then add the mussels, cockles and prawns. Toss well in the butter, sprinkle with pepper and lemon juice and heat through. Serve hot, topped with plenty of parsley and hand lemon butter separately. Serve with brown bread and butter.

Super 'star'
winners with the kids

Children are changing their tastes in party food. Savouries are now far more popular than sweets, especially with the older kids, and for teenage parties sausages are essential, while bland jellies are often left uneaten.

The sweet things which are enjoyed are more likely to be mousses, creams and cakes with fun toppings, rather than a sponge sandwich with pink icing. But there's no change in the enjoyment of novel newcomers, like Chocolate cheesecake in a crumb crust. On the other hand, Gingerbread men have an eternal appeal.

Some children get so excited at parties they can hardly eat at all. For nibblers, Savoury cheese straws are just right, and a rather economical yet rich-tasting home-made ice cream always slips down easily when sandwiches loom too large and stodgy. I have a theory that a daunting wedge of birthday cake is often refused for the same reason. Why not cut up some slices into 'tasters' and put them on a plate to be handed round, so all the young guests can wish the birthday boy or girl good luck?

A gaily set table is exciting to the eyes of youngsters who often eat in a hurry in the kitchen, but everything ought to be disposable or easy to wash. When good spirits get a bit wild, that's when a playful race to get the last sausage on a stick may send another plate of goodies sliding across the table, upsetting everything else in its path, a plastic cloth under a brightly coloured washable one makes such accidents less damaging to your table. There are now delightful designs in disposable paper cloths (once so tasteless and garish). A bit expensive, but it might save mother's time and a headache, is to use matching cloth, napkins, beakers and plates. Plastic cutlery I find less successful, it seems more difficult to manipulate with small, eager hands than a good solid metal spoon or fork. Provide plenty of extra paper napkins in the background to mop up any spills. Don't be disappointed if youngsters refuse the iced birthday cake, although it is there to be admired and for the ceremony of blowing out the candles, at least until the age of eight. After that, the candles seem less cute, and the pride in their number diminishes! But there are lots of other parties ahead – bonfire night, exam-passing celebrations, team victories, or just an evening's fun for a group of boys and girls all about the same age as your child. With these parties in mind, I have chosen a batch of rather more sophisticated recipes, all of which look fun to eat and are not too expensive to produce. The drinks favoured are mostly the fizzy kind, from colas and pops for the tinies to cider, mildly alcoholic punches and cups for teenagers. Hot soups and hot chocolate drunk from a mug seem to please too, especially for outdoor gatherings like firework shows and evening barbecues. I have put barbecues in this section because once you've rustled up a good, tasty barbecue sauce, the foods are simple. There is a rather nice selection of basic barbecue foods to be basted with a zingy sauce. Provide soft bap rolls to put the cooked food inside, dishes of mustard, pickles and relishes for individual improvements, and baked potatoes to slit open and fill with butter.

Hallowe'en party plan (pages 72–73): witch's hot dogs, magic potatoes, party bread, Hallowe'en soup and windmill salad.

Savoury cheese straws

Preparation time 10 minutes plus 1 hour chilling time
Cooking time 8–10 minutes
Makes about 25

IMPERIAL/METRIC	AMERICAN
2 oz./50 g. unsalted butter	¼ cup sweet butter
1 oz./25 g. Cheddar cheese, grated	¼ cup grated Cheddar cheese
3 oz./75 g. plain flour	¾ cup all-purpose flour
pinch cayenne pepper	pinch cayenne pepper
¼ teaspoon salt	¼ teaspoon salt
1 teaspoon vegetable extract	1 teaspoon savory spread
1 egg yolk	1 egg yolk

Chill a mixing bowl and prepare the straws in cool conditions. Place the butter, cheese, flour and seasoning in the bowl and rub in the butter. Dissolve the vegetable extract in 5 teaspoons of boiling water. Beat the egg yolk and add to the water and vegetable extract, blending well. Pour into the cheese mixture in the bowl and mix well. Mould lightly into a round shape, dust with flour and chill in the refrigerator for 1 hour.

Place the dough on a floured board and roll into a rectangle $\frac{1}{16}$ inch (0·25 cm.) thick. Using a pastry wheel or sharp knife, cut into strips about ½ inch (1 cm.) wide and 4 inches (10 cm.) long. Place the straws on an ungreased baking sheet and cook in the centre of a moderately hot oven (400°F., 200°C., Gas Mark 6) until straw coloured. Cool on a wire rack.

Mince surprise

Preparation time 30 minutes
Cooking time 30 minutes
Serves 4–6

IMPERIAL/METRIC	AMERICAN
8 oz./225 g. macaroni	½ lb. macaroni
1 small onion	1 small onion
2 oz./50 g. butter	¼ cup butter
8 oz./225 g. minced beef	1 cup ground beef
1 (7-oz./200-g.) can tomatoes	1 (7-oz.) can tomatoes
salt and pepper	salt and pepper
pinch dried herbs	pinch dried herbs
few drops Worcestershire sauce	few drops Worcestershire sauce
sauce	**sauce**
2 oz./50 g. butter	¼ cup butter
1½ oz./40 g. flour	6 tablespoons all-purpose flour
¾ pint/4 dl. milk	2 cups milk
2 oz./50 g. Lancashire cheese, grated	½ cup grated cheese

Cook the macaroni in a large pan of boiling salted water for about 12–15 minutes, until tender. Meanwhile, chop the onion finely. Melt 1½ oz. (40 g., 3 tablespoons) butter in a frying pan and use to cook the onion until soft but not coloured. Stir in the minced beef and fry until browned, breaking the meat down with a fork. Stir from time to time to prevent the meat sticking. Add the tomatoes, salt, pepper, herbs and Worcestershire sauce. Stir again and cook for 10 minutes.

To make the sauce, melt the butter in a saucepan and stir in the flour. Cook for 2 minutes. Gradually blend in the milk and bring to the boil, stirring constantly, until the sauce is thick and smooth. Stir in half the grated cheese.

Drain the cooked macaroni thoroughly and toss with the remaining ½ oz. (10 g., 1 tablespoon) butter. Turn half the macaroni into an ovenproof dish and cover with half the cheese sauce. Add the mince mixture and cover this with the rest of the macaroni. Finally pour over the remaining sauce and sprinkle with the rest of the grated cheese. Place in a moderately hot oven (375°F., 190°C., Gas Mark 5) for 30 minutes, until the cheese on the top has melted and become a golden brown.

Spaghetti with party sauce

Preparation time 10 minutes
Cooking time 55 minutes
Serves 4

IMPERIAL/METRIC	AMERICAN
12 oz./350 g. spaghetti	¾ lb. spaghetti
1 oz./25 g. butter	2 tablespoons butter
freshly ground black pepper	freshly ground black pepper
1 oz./25 g. cheese, grated (preferably Parmesan)	¼ cup grated cheese (preferably Parmesan)
sauce	**sauce**
1 large onion	1 large onion
1 carrot	1 carrot
1 stick celery	1 stalk celery
3 tablespoons oil	¼ cup oil
2 oz./50 g. lean minced beef	¼ cup lean ground beef
8 oz./225 g. chicken livers, chopped	1 cup chopped chicken livers
1 (10-oz./275-g.) can tomatoes	1 (10-oz.) can tomatoes
½ pint/3 dl. stock	1¼ cups stock
1 bay leaf	1 bay leaf
½ teaspoon dried oregano	½ teaspoon dried oregano
3 tablespoons tomato purée	¼ cup tomato paste
salt and black pepper	salt and black pepper

To make the sauce, finely chop the onion, carrot and celery. Heat the oil in a frying pan and use to fry the vegetables gently until golden brown. Add the minced beef and chopped chicken livers and cook until brown.

Turn the mixture into a saucepan and add the remaining ingredients. Stir well and cook for 45 minutes, stirring from time to time.

Fifteen minutes before the sauce is ready, cook the spaghetti in plenty of boiling salted water, for about 12 minutes or as directed on the packet. Drain the spaghetti and melt a knob of butter in the saucepan. Return the spaghetti to the saucepan, toss in melted butter and sprinkle with freshly ground black pepper. Serve on hot plates with the sauce spooned on top and hand grated cheese separately. For special occasions, add a spoonful of cream to the sauce before serving.

Beef bubble and squeak

Preparation time 10 minutes
Cooking time 10 minutes
Serves 4

IMPERIAL/METRIC	AMERICAN
6 slices corned beef	6 slices corned beef
3 tablespoons butter or oil	4 tablespoons butter or oil
1 lb./450 g. chopped cabbage, boiled	6 cups chopped cabbage, boiled
1 lb./450 g. mashed potatoes or 1 packet instant potato serving 4	1 lb. mashed potatoes or 1 package instant potato serving 4
1 tablespoon vinegar	1 tablespoon vinegar
salt and pepper	salt and pepper

Have the meat sliced thinly, or chop it into pieces. Heat the butter or oil until smoking hot, reduce the heat then fry the corned beef until golden brown. Remove the meat to a dish and keep hot.

Mix the chopped cabbage and potatoes together and heat in the butter or oil. Add the vinegar and season to taste. Heat through thoroughly and allow to brown slightly. Remove to a hot dish and arrange overlapping slices of corned beef round. Alternatively, fork the chopped corned beef round the edge.

Sausage and bacon jacket potatoes

Preparation time 15 minutes
Cooking time 1½–2 hours
Serves 5

IMPERIAL/METRIC	AMERICAN
5 large potatoes	5 large potatoes
3 oz./75 g. butter	6 tablespoons butter
4 tablespoons milk	⅓ cup milk
4 rashers lean bacon	4 lean bacon slices
4 skinless sausages	4 skinless sausages
2 tablespoons cream cheese	3 tablespoons cream cheese
salt and pepper	salt and pepper
2 oz./50 g. cheese, grated	½ cup grated cheese

Prick the potatoes with a fork and bake in a moderately hot oven (400°F., 200°C., Gas Mark 6) for 1½–2 hours, until soft. When cooked, cut them in half, then scoop out the soft insides and mash with two-thirds of the butter and the milk.

While the potatoes are cooking, derind the bacon and fry with the sausages until crisp, then chop into small pieces. Add the cream cheese, chopped sausage and bacon to the potato mixture and mix well. Season well and use to fill the potato cases. Sprinkle with grated cheese, dot with the remaining butter and grill until golden. Serve as a teatime dish with grilled tomatoes and/or mushrooms.

Flying saucers

Preparation time 5 minutes
Cooking time 10 minutes
Serves 4

IMPERIAL/METRIC	AMERICAN
4 large slices of bread	4 large slices of bread
3 oz./75 g. butter	6 tablespoons butter
4 eggs	4 eggs
salt and pepper	salt and pepper
4 oz./100 g. cheese, grated	1 cup grated cheese

Toast the bread lightly and cut into rounds, then cut holes in the centre to fit the eggs. Spread the toasted rounds with butter and place in a buttered ovenproof dish. Melt the remaining butter in a saucepan. Break an egg into the centre of each piece of toast and sprinkle with seasoning. Pour a little of the melted butter on top of each egg, then cover with grated cheese. Bake in a moderate oven (325°F., 160°C., Gas Mark 3) for 10 minutes, until the egg white is set.

Gingernut whip

Preparation time 15 minutes plus chilling time
Serves 4

IMPERIAL/METRIC	AMERICAN
1 (11-oz./315-g.) can pineapple cubes	1 (11-oz.) can pineapple cubes
16 gingernut biscuits	16 ginger snaps
½ (2½-oz./65-g.) pineapple jelly	½ package pineapple-flavored gelatin
1 small can evaporated milk	1 small can evaporated milk
to decorate	**to decorate**
stem ginger or pineapple	stem ginger or pineapple

Drain the pineapple cubes, reserving the juice, and cut the cubes in half. Dip the ginger biscuits in the pineapple juice and place round the sides of four glass serving dishes. Make up the jelly to ½ pint (3 dl., 1¼ cups) with boiling water and allow to cool. Just before the jelly starts to set, whip in the evaporated milk until a light fluffy mixture is obtained. For speed, use a rotary beater or electric mixer. Place some chopped pineapple cubes in the bottom of each dish and pour the jelly whip on top. Decorate each one with slices of ginger or pineapple pieces. This sweet can also be made in a glass soufflé dish or glass bowl. Chill well.

Banana crunchies

Preparation time 10–15 minutes
Cooking time 15 minutes
Makes about 5 dozen

IMPERIAL/METRIC	AMERICAN
6 oz./175 g. plain flour	1½ cups all-purpose flour
8 oz./225 g. castor sugar	1 cup sugar
½ teaspoon bicarbonate of soda	½ teaspoon baking soda
1 teaspoon salt	1 teaspoon salt
¼ teaspoon nutmeg	¼ teaspoon nutmeg
1 teaspoon cinnamon	1 teaspoon cinnamon
6 oz./175 g. butter	¾ cup butter
1 egg	1 egg
3 ripe bananas	3 ripe bananas
4 oz./100 g. rolled oats	generous cup rolled oats
1 oz./25 g. nuts, chopped	¼ cup chopped nuts

Sieve the flour, sugar, bicarbonate of soda, salt, nutmeg and cinnamon together in a bowl. Rub the butter into the dry ingredients until the mixture resembles fine breadcrumbs. Add the beaten egg, mashed bananas, rolled oats and nuts and mix all ingredients well. Put teaspoons of the mixture on greased baking sheets, allowing space for spreading. Bake in a moderately hot oven (375°F., 190°C., Gas Mark 5) for about 15 minutes. When cooked, leave on the baking trays for 1–2 minutes before removing to cool on a wire rack.

Peach toffee crumble

Preparation 10 minutes
Cooking time 30 minutes
Serves 6

IMPERIAL/METRIC	AMERICAN
1 (16-oz./450-g.) can peach halves	1 (16-oz.) can peach halves
1 tablespoon sultanas	1 tablespoon seedless white raisins
4 tablespoons soft brown sugar	⅓ cup soft brown sugar
4 oz./100 g. flour	1 cup all-purpose flour
2 oz./50 g. butter	¼ cup butter
¼ pint/1½ dl. double cream	⅔ cup whipping cream
3 tablespoons demerara sugar	¼ cup brown sugar

Drain the peaches, reserve one and place the remainder in the bottom of an ovenproof dish. Sprinkle with the sultanas and soft brown sugar. Place the flour in a bowl and rub in the butter until mixture resembles breadcrumbs. Sprinkle on top of the peaches and brown sugar and cook in a moderate oven (350°F., 180°C., Gas Mark 4) for 30 minutes.

Remove from the oven, pour over the cream and sprinkle with demerara sugar. Grill until the sugar melts. Decorate with the reserved, sliced peach half.

Banana butterscotch

Preparation time 15 minutes
Serves 4

IMPERIAL/METRIC	AMERICAN
2 ripe bananas	2 ripe bananas
1 tablespoon sugar	1 tablespoon sugar
2 tablespoons lemon juice	3 tablespoons lemon juice
1 packet instant butterscotch dessert	1 package instant butterscotch pudding
1 pint/6 dl. milk	2½ cups milk
1 oz./25 g. walnuts, chopped	¼ cup chopped walnuts
topping	**topping**
2 bananas	2 bananas
1 tablespoon lemon juice	1 tablespoon lemon juice
4 walnut halves	4 walnut halves

Mash the ripe bananas with the sugar and lemon juice, then divide between four glass dessert dishes or place in one medium-sized glass bowl. Make up the butterscotch dessert with the milk, stirring in the chopped walnuts. Pour on to the mashed bananas and allow to set for a few minutes. Cut the other two bananas into slices and dip them in lemon juice. Decorate the top of the butterscotch dessert with the sliced bananas and walnut halves.

Chocolate ginger drops

Preparation time 15 minutes
Makes 30

IMPERIAL/METRIC	AMERICAN
6 ginger biscuits	6 ginger snaps
8 oz./225 g. chocolate	½ lb. chocolate
4 tablespoons evaporated milk	5 tablespoons evaporated milk
4 tablespoons icing sugar	5 tablespoons sifted confectioners' sugar
4 tablespoons chopped nuts	5 tablespoons chopped nuts
½ teaspoon vanilla essence	½ teaspoon vanilla extract

Crush the ginger biscuits with a rolling pin or put them into a liquidiser. Melt the chocolate in a large bowl over hot water then add the biscuit crumbs, evaporated milk, icing sugar, nuts and vanilla essence. Mix thoroughly and put teaspoons of the mixture on a sheet of oiled greaseproof paper. Flatten slightly and firm in the refrigerator. Peel away from the paper and put the drops in small paper cases.

Gingerbread men

Preparation time 15 minutes
Cooking time about 10 minutes
Makes about 10

IMPERIAL/METRIC	AMERICAN
2 oz./50 g. butter	¼ cup butter
2 oz./50 g. castor sugar	¼ cup sugar
1 tablespoon black treacle	1 tablespoon black molasses
4 oz./100 g. self-raising flour	1 cup all-purpose flour with 1 teaspoon baking powder
1 teaspoon ground ginger	1 teaspoon ground ginger
¼ teaspoon mixed spice	¼ teaspoon mixed spice
milk to mix	milk to mix

Cream the butter and sugar together until light and fluffy, then mix in the treacle and beat well. Sieve the flour, ginger and mixed spice on to the mixture and fold in with a metal spoon. Add a little milk if the mixture seems to be too stiff. Turn out on to a floured board and knead before rolling out thinly to about ⅛ inch (0·25 cm.) thickness. Using a metal cutter or the cardboard cut-out of a man, cut out the gingerbread men; re-kneading scraps, and re-rolling. Lift the gingerbread men carefully and place on a greased baking tray. Bake in the centre of a moderate oven (350°F., 180°C., Gas Mark 4) for 7–10 minutes. Leave the gingerbread men on the baking sheet for 3–4 minutes before transferring them to a wire cooling rack. Decorate with currants, icing or sweets.

Chocolate cheesecake

Preparation time 25 minutes
Cooking time 5 minutes
Serves 6

IMPERIAL/METRIC	AMERICAN
4 oz./100 g. digestive biscuits	¼ lb. graham crackers
2 oz./50 g. butter	¼ cup butter
2 oz./50 g. soft brown sugar	¼ cup soft brown sugar
filling	**filling**
8 oz./225 g. cream cheese	1 cup cream cheese
4 oz./100 g. castor sugar	½ cup sugar
4 oz./100 g. plain chocolate	¼ lb. semi-sweet chocolate
2 eggs	2 eggs
½ pint/3 dl. double cream	1¼ cups whipping cream

Crush the biscuits with a rolling pin between two sheets of greaseproof paper. Melt the butter and stir in the sugar and crushed biscuits. Press the mixture into a 10-inch (26-cm.) pie plate and chill.

To make the filling, put the cream cheese in a bowl and beat well until smooth, then beat in half the sugar. Melt the chocolate in a bowl over hot water, allow to cool slightly and beat into the cream cheese mixture. Separate the eggs and add the egg yolks to the chocolate mixture. Beat the egg whites until stiff and fold in the remaining castor sugar. Lightly whip the cream and fold in the egg whites carefully, using a metal spoon. Next, fold most of the cream into the chocolate mixture, but reserve enough to decorate the top with piped rosettes. Turn the mixture into the prepared biscuit crust and chill in the refrigerator. Whip the remaining cream until it is thick and pipe or spoon on top of the cheesecake.

Strawberry ice cream

Preparation time 15 minutes plus chilling and
freezing time
Makes 2 pints (1 litre, 5 cups)

IMPERIAL/METRIC	AMERICAN
1 (14-oz./400-g.) can evaporated milk	1 (14-oz.) can evaporated milk
2 tablespoons cornflour	3 tablespoons cornstarch
¼ pint/1½ dl. water	⅔ cup water
3 oz./75 g. sugar	6 tablespoons sugar
1 lb./450 g. packet frozen strawberries, defrosted	1 lb. package frozen strawberries, defrosted

Put half the evaporated milk in the freezing compartment of the refrigerator until very cold. Blend the cornflour until smooth with a little of the measured water. Beat in the remainder of the milk, sugar and water with an electric beater or whisk for about 10 seconds. Pour into a saucepan and cook over medium heat until thick. Cool and chill.

Remove the icy cold evaporated milk from the refrigerator and whip with an electric beater until it is stiff. Add the chilled cornflour mixture and whisk well, cleaning down the sides of the bowl with a spatula. Sieve or liquidise the strawberries, stir into the mixture. Pour into ice trays or a 1-lb. (½-kg.) loaf tin and freeze. If you are making the ice cream in the freezing compartment of the refrigerator, take it out after about 30 minutes and stir round; this helps the mixture to freeze evenly.

Vanilla fudge

Preparation time 5 minutes
Cooking time 10–15 minutes
Makes about 48 squares

IMPERIAL/METRIC	AMERICAN
2 tablespoons golden syrup	3 tablespoons corn syrup
3 tablespoons water	¼ cup water
3 oz./75 g. butter or margarine	6 tablespoons butter or margarine
1 lb./450 g. castor sugar	2 cups sugar
1 small can condensed milk	1 small can sweetened condensed milk
few drops vanilla essence	few drops vanilla extract

Put the golden syrup, water, butter and castor sugar into a heavy-based saucepan. Heat slowly until the sugar has dissolved, then add the condensed milk and bring to the boil, stirring. Continue boiling the mixture for 10–15 minutes, stirring constantly, until it is a golden brown. At this point a small amount dropped into cold water should form a soft ball. Remove from the heat and beat until thick before adding the vanilla essence. Pour the mixture into a lightly greased tin about 8 × 12 inches (20 × 31 cm.) in size. Mark the fudge into squares with a knife when half set. Do not remove from the tin until cold.

Orange and chocolate cup cakes

Preparation time 20 minutes
Cooking time 20 minutes
Makes about 15

IMPERIAL/METRIC	AMERICAN
4 oz./100 g. butter	½ cup butter
4 oz./100 g. castor sugar	½ cup sugar
zest of 1 orange	zest of 1 orange
juice of ½ orange	juice of ½ orange
2 eggs, beaten	2 eggs, beaten
4 oz./100 g. self-raising flour	1 cup all-purpose flour sifted with 1 teaspoon baking powder
½ packet chocolate chips	½ package chocolate chips
icing	**icing**
2 oz./50 g. butter	¼ cup butter
4 oz./100 g. icing sugar	1 cup confectioners' sugar
juice of ½ orange	juice of ½ orange
1 drop of red food colouring (optional)	1 drop of red food coloring (optional)
to decorate	**to decorate**
chocolate chips	chocolate chips

Cream the butter and sugar until light and fluffy. Add the orange zest and juice and mix thoroughly. Gradually add the eggs, beating well between each addition and adding 1 teaspoon of flour if liked, to prevent curdling. Fold in the sieved flour with a metal spoon. Add the chocolate chips and mix gently. Spoon the mixture into paper cases which have been lightly dusted with flour. Cook on the centre shelf of a moderate oven (350°F., 180°C., Gas Mark 4) for 20 minutes. Cool on a wire rack.

To make the butter icing, beat the butter until soft and creamy. Add the sieved icing sugar a little at a time until smooth. Add the orange juice and the colouring, if used. Decorate each cake with butter icing and three chocolate chips. Alternatively, decorate with sugared orange slices.

Mocha butterflies

Preparation time 20 minutes
Cooking time 20 minutes
Makes 10

IMPERIAL/METRIC	AMERICAN
2 oz./50 g. butter	¼ cup butter
2 oz./50 g. castor sugar	¼ cup sugar
1 egg	1 egg
2 oz./50 g. self-raising flour	½ cup all-purpose flour sifted with ½ teaspoon baking powder
1 tablespoon milk	1 tablespoon milk
few drops vanilla essence	few drops vanilla extract
1½ teaspoons coffee essence	1½ teaspoons coffee extract
1 teaspoon cocoa powder	1 teaspoon unsweetened cocoa powder
filling	**filling**
¼ pint/1½ dl. double cream	⅔ cup whipping cream
2 teaspoons castor sugar	2 teaspoons sugar

Cream the butter until soft, add the sugar and beat until the mixture is light and fluffy. Lightly beat the egg and add it together with a tablespoon of flour. Stir, then beat briskly. Add the milk, vanilla essence and a little more flour, then the coffee essence. Sieve the cocoa into the remaining flour and fold into the mixture. Half fill ten baking cases and bake in a moderately hot oven (375°F., 190°C., Gas Mark 5) for 15–20 minutes. Cool on a wire rack.

To make the filling, whip the double cream with the sugar. When the cakes are cold, cut a slice off the top of each cake and fill with piped rosettes of cream. Cut the cake tops in half and decorate by placing on the filling with the rounded edges facing outwards.

Treacle toffee

Preparation time 5 minutes
Cooking time 10 minutes
Makes about 12 oz./350 g.

IMPERIAL/METRIC	AMERICAN
4 oz./100 g. butter	½ cup butter
8 oz./225 g. granulated sugar	1 cup sugar
3 tablespoons black treacle	¼ cup molasses
2 tablespoons vinegar	3 tablespoons vinegar

Melt the butter in a large saucepan, adding all the ingredients and stirring continuously until the sugar has dissolved. Bring to the boil and allow to boil briskly for about 10 minutes. The toffee is ready when a little of the mixture forms a firm ball if dropped into cold water. Pour into a greased 7-inch (18-cm.) square tin and mark into squares while still warm. Break into pieces when cold.

Toffee apples

Preparation time 10 minutes
Cooking time about 10 minutes
Makes 6–8

IMPERIAL/METRIC	AMERICAN
1 lb./450 g. castor sugar	2 cups sugar, firmly packed
2 oz./50 g. butter	¼ cup butter
1½ teaspoons vinegar	1½ teaspoons vinegar
¼ pint/1½ dl. water	⅔ cup water
1 tablespoon golden syrup	1 tablespoon corn syrup
6–8 medium eating apples	6–8 medium eating apples

Place the sugar, butter, vinegar, water and syrup into a large, heavy-based saucepan. Heat gently until the sugar has dissolved, then boil rapidly for 5 minutes or until the temperature reaches 290°F., (145°C.). Wipe the apples with a clean damp cloth, push wooden sticks into the cores. Dip the apples into the toffee until completely coated. Leave to set on a baking tray or waxed paper.

Barbecue party plan

A barbecue is a popular summer entertainment for children of all ages, but younger ones do need an adult to supervise cooking operations, with tongs for turning, lots of oven mitts, cloths, soft kitchen paper. Apart from cutlets, which can be held with a small twist of paper round the bone, other items, such as sausages and thick bacon rashers, should be popped into soft baps, soft long rolls or between toasted bread slices. Baste generously throughout cooking with the following sauce.

Barbecue sauce

Preparation time 5 minutes
Cooking time about 25 minutes

Heat the oil in a saucepan and use to fry the onion and bacon until transparent. Add the remaining ingredients, except the arrowroot, and bring to the boil, stirring constantly. Simmer for 20 minutes, then remove from the heat. Blend the arrowroot with 2 tablespoons water and stir into the sauce. Bring to the boil, stirring, cook for 2 minutes.

IMPERIAL/METRIC	AMERICAN
1 tablespoon oil	1 tablespoon oil
2 medium onions, chopped	2 medium onions, chopped
1 rasher streaky bacon, chopped	1 bacon slice, chopped
1 tablespoon tomato purée	1 tablespoon tomato paste
½ pint/3 dl. cider	1¼ cups cider
2 oz./50 g. demerara sugar	¼ cup brown sugar
2 teaspoons Worcestershire sauce	2 teaspoons Worcestershire sauce
1 tablespoon sweet chutney	1 tablespoon sweet chutney or relish
salt and pepper to taste	salt and pepper to taste
1 teaspoon arrowroot	1 teaspoon arrowroot flour

Hallowe'en party plan

ILLUSTRATED IN COLOUR ON PAGE 63

If there's one party teenagers enjoy, it's at Hallowe'en with its atmosphere of magic and mysterious predictions for the future. The same recipes are ideal for a gathering of younger children on Guy Fawkes night, with hot chocolate instead of beer and wine!
This menu would be acceptable in or out of doors.

Witch's hot dogs

Preparation time 5 minutes
Cooking time about 10 minutes
Serves 6

IMPERIAL/METRIC	AMERICAN
6 rashers streaky bacon	6 bacon slices
1 teaspoon made mustard	1 teaspoon prepared mustard
6 frankfurter sausages	6 frankfurters
6 oz./175 g. Gouda cheese	⅓ lb. Dutch cheese
3 long bread rolls	3 long bread rolls

Derind the bacon and fry gently until just cooked. Slit the sausages lengthways and spread the cut surfaces with the made mustard. Cut half of the cheese into strips ¼ inch (0·5 cm.) wide and use to fill the sausages. Wrap a rasher of bacon round each filled sausage and secure with a cocktail stick. Cut the remaining cheese into 6 slices. Cut the bread rolls in half and place a slice of cheese on each half. Sprinkle with cayenne pepper, if liked, and top each with a sausage. Place under a hot grill for 5 minutes.

Windmill salad

Preparation time 5 minutes
Serves 4

Cut the tomatoes into wedges and place in a salad bowl with the lettuce leaves, cucumber slices and cheese cubes. Just before serving, toss in dressing.

IMPERIAL/METRIC	AMERICAN
3 tomatoes	3 tomatoes
1 large lettuce	1 large lettuce
¼ cucumber, sliced	¼ cucumber, sliced
6 oz./175 g. Edam cheese, cubed	1 cup cubed Dutch cheese
French dressing (see page 51)	French dressing (see page 51)

Hallowe'en soup

Preparation time 10 minutes
Cooking time about 25 minutes
Serves 4–6

Melt the butter and use to cook the onion, leek and cauliflower gently in a covered pan for about 10–15 minutes, until soft. Add the sliced carrots. Stir in the flour with a wooden spoon and cook for 2–3 minutes. Dissolve the stock cubes in the boiling water, add to the vegetables and bring to the boil, stirring constantly. Add the chopped frankfurters and simmer for 10 minutes. Season to taste with salt, pepper and a dash of Worcestershire sauce. Just before serving, add the parsley and grated cheese.

IMPERIAL/METRIC	AMERICAN
2 oz./50 g. butter	¼ cup butter
2 onions, chopped	2 onions, chopped
1 leek, chopped	1 leek, chopped
1 small cauliflower, in sprigs	1 small cauliflower, in sprigs
1 (8-oz./225-g.) can carrots, sliced	1 (8-oz.) can carrots, sliced
2 oz./50 g. plain flour	½ cup all-purpose flour
2 chicken stock cubes	2 chicken bouillon cubes
1½ pints/scant litre boiling water	3¾ cups boiling water
1 (8-oz./225-g.) can frankfurters, drained	1 (8-oz.) can frankfurters, drained
salt and pepper	salt and pepper
dash Worcestershire sauce	dash Worcestershire sauce
2 tablespoons chopped parsley	3 tablespoons chopped parsley
2 oz./50 g. Gouda cheese, grated	½ cup grated Dutch cheese

Party bread

Preparation time 10 minutes
Cooking time about 30 minutes
Serves 8

IMPERIAL/METRIC	AMERICAN
1 small French loaf	1 small French loaf
4 oz./100 g. butter	½ cup butter
8 oz./225 g. minced beef	1 cup ground beef, firmly packed
1 onion, chopped	1 onion, chopped
2 tablespoons tomato purée	3 tablespoons tomato paste
pinch mixed herbs	pinch mixed herbs
salt, pepper and ground nutmeg to taste	salt, pepper and ground nutmeg to taste
to garnish	**to garnish**
8 thin triangles of Gouda cheese (approx. 6 oz./175 g.)	8 thin triangles of Dutch cheese (approx. 6 oz.)
8 tomato slices	8 tomato slices

Slice the French loaf in half lengthways and scoop out the soft centre. Use 3 oz. (75 g.) of this soft bread to make breadcrumbs. Melt half the butter and use to brush the inside of the scooped out loaf. Melt the remaining butter in a frying pan and use to cook the minced beef and onion for 10 minutes. Add the tomato purée, herbs, seasonings and breadcrumbs. Fill the scooped out loaf with the meat mixture and place in a moderate oven (350°F., 180°C., Gas Mark 4) for 15–20 minutes. Serve hot, garnished with triangles of cheese and slices of tomato.

Magic potatoes

Preparation time 10 minutes
Cooking time about 1 hour 40 minutes
Serves 4

IMPERIAL/METRIC	AMERICAN
4 medium potatoes	4 medium potatoes
1 oz./25 g. butter	2 tablespoons butter
2 oz./50 g. onion, chopped	½ cup chopped onion
4 oz./100 g. mushrooms, sliced	1 cup sliced mushrooms
4 oz./100 g. Gouda cheese	1 cup grated Dutch cheese

Scrub the potatoes and prick with a fork. Place on a baking sheet in a hot oven (425°F., 220°C., Gas Mark 7) for about 1–1½ hours, until soft. Meanwhile, melt the butter and use to fry the onion and mushroom slices until soft. When the potatoes are cooked, cut in half lengthways, scoop out the soft centres and mash with three-quarters of the grated cheese, onion, mushroom and seasoning. Place back in the shell and place under the grill until heated through. Sprinkle with remaining grated cheese and garnish with parsley sprigs. Keep hot and serve with a mixed salad.

Elegant menus
to delight your guests

Composing a dinner party menu is one of those delightful tasks which gives your imagination full rein. It is more important that the meal should be perfectly balanced than elaborate. Each course should introduce a change of flavour, texture and colour. Never follow brown Windsor soup by stewed oxtail! Nor offer a white fish mousse as hors d'oeuvre, followed by breast of chicken in a cream sauce with rice, concluding with a vanilla bavarois for dessert.

Fruity or fishy starters, served cold, are pretty and easy to prepare ahead. A cold consommé, if really well set, looks and tastes good. Hot soups are easy too, because if made in advance, they seem to improve in flavour when reheated. A word of warning – transfer the soup to a heated jug with a good pouring lip rather than pouring from the pan. Splashes round a soup coupe or plate look ugly, and when one is hurried and a trifle nervous, this accident happens all too easily. Hot consommé from a can benefits enormously from a dose of dry sherry (1 tablespoon per serving) and a sprinkling on top of chopped parsley or tiny peeled shrimps.

The choice of main course is governed by the amount of time and effort you can spare just before serving time. Casseroled dishes, which are cooked by the time the guests arrive and can then be left firmly covered in a low oven until needed, are easiest of all. The most demanding are grills or fried dishes which must be cooked at the last moment, almost guaranteeing a tiresome wait, strong odours wafting from the kitchen, and some unwanted stains on your best dress. A dish to be served with panache on a big platter might be based on rice (saffron, savoury or brown rice for a change) or on pasta – white and green ribbon noodles are fine. Chicken joints, fillets of fish, slices of meat can rest on this bed, which forms a pretty border, and this is easy to garnish further with button mushrooms, halved tomatoes, or parsley sprigs. Over the food pour just an introductory trickle of the sauce you intend to serve, or occasionally a complete mask of sauce, with an eye-catching stuffed olive or green sprig on top. Parsley and watercress are simplest, and more of the same can be incorporated in a green salad. Extra sauce to hand round the table is essential, for some guests prefer more sauce than others, and as it is bound to be tempting, make plenty.

Remember, a most important quality for dinner party food is for it to be assembled at serving time, looking fresh, moist, glistening and really hot. Food dried out in the oven, or cooled down to faintly warm, never tastes as nice.

These days the starter, main course and sweet are usually extended by serving a cheese and fruit platter instead of a traditional savoury. If you are drinking red wine, it is now the custom to serve cheese first and finish up the wine before tackling the sweet. Unless this includes a fruit salad or lots of fruit in some other form, I decorate the cheese board with fruit; small clusters of grapes, particularly choice apples or pears, or a wreath of mandarin slices round a whole Camembert. Something exotic (such as Chinese gooseberries, early white cherries, balls of Charentais melon) goes with cheese and is more memorable than the ever-acceptable celery.

Fondue bourguignonne (pages 90–91) with tomato relish, corn relish, curry sauce, béarnaise sauce and pepper and onion relish.

Bortsch

Preparation time 15 minutes
Cooking time about 1 hour 10 minutes
Serves 4

IMPERIAL/METRIC	AMERICAN
2 medium onions	2 medium onions
1 tablespoon oil	1 tablespoon oil
3 beetroots	3 beets
6 oz./175 g. cabbage, chopped	2¼ cups chopped cabbage
1¼ pints/7½ dl. stock	3 cups stock
2 tablespoons vinegar	3 tablespoons vinegar
¼ teaspoon salt	¼ teaspoon salt
pepper	pepper
¼ pint/1½ dl. soured cream	⅔ cup sour cream
to garnish	**to garnish**
chopped chives	chopped chives

Chop the onions finely and cook gently in the oil, in a large saucepan, until soft but not brown. Peel the beetroot, chop roughly and add to the onion. Add the remaining ingredients except the cream, bring to the boil and simmer gently for 1 hour in a covered pan. Rub through a sieve or blend in a liquidiser. Return to the pan and heat, adding water or stock if the soup is too thick. Divide the soured cream between the bowls of soup, trickling on top of the soup. Garnish with chopped chives.

New Orleans jambalaya

Preparation time 20–25 minutes
Cooking time 30–35 minutes
Serves 4

IMPERIAL/METRIC	AMERICAN
2 oz./50 g. butter	¼ cup butter
1 medium green pepper, chopped	1 medium green sweet pepper, chopped
2 medium onions, chopped	2 medium onions, chopped
1 clove garlic, crushed	1 clove garlic, crushed
1 lb./450 g. potatoes, diced	1 lb. potatoes, diced
6 oz./175 g. long grain rice	scant cup long grain rice
8 oz./225 g. frankfurters	½ lb. frankfurters
12 oz./350 g. ham, diced	1½ cups diced cooked cured ham
4-oz./100-g. packet frozen prawns	¼-lb. package frozen shrimp or prawns
1 pint/6 dl. chicken stock	2½ cups chicken stock
1 bay leaf	1 bay leaf
¼ teaspoon dried thyme	¼ teaspoon dried thyme
1 teaspoon Tabasco sauce	1 teaspoon Tabasco sauce
salt and pepper	salt and pepper
1 tablespoon chopped parsley	1 tablespoon chopped parsley

Melt the butter in a large frying pan. Add the pepper, onion and garlic, and fry gently until the onions are tender, but not brown. Add the potatoes and rice and cook for a minute, stirring all the time. Next add the frankfurters, ham, prawns, stock, bay leaf, thyme, Tabasco sauce and seasoning. Bring to the boil, stirring gently, and cook for about 5 minutes. Turn into an ovenproof dish, cover and cook in a moderately hot oven (375°F., 190°C., Gas Mark 5) for 30–35 minutes, or until the rice and potatoes are tender. Remove from the oven, remove the bay leaf and sprinkle the jambalaya with parsley. Serve hot.

Rich raspberry ice cream

Preparation time 15 minutes plus freezing time
Serves 4

IMPERIAL/METRIC	AMERICAN
¾ pint/4 dl. single cream	2 cups coffee cream
2½ oz./65 g. castor sugar	5 tablespoons sugar
4 tablespoons water	⅓ cup water
3 egg yolks	3 egg yolks
½ pint/3 dl. raspberry purée	1¼ cups raspberry purée

Heat cream in a pan over a low heat until almost at boiling point. Boil the sugar and water together until almost a syrup. Whisk the egg yolks and pour into the syrup, whisking all the time until the mixture becomes very thick. Add the heated cream and then the raspberry purée. Put in freezer trays, cover and freeze for about 40 minutes. Turn back into the bowl, whisk well then freeze completely. Scoop into dishes.

MENU
Frosty cucumber soup
Eastern beef
Blackberry and apple summer gnocchi

Frosty cucumber soup

Preparation time 10 minutes plus standing time
Serves 4

IMPERIAL/METRIC	AMERICAN
1 cucumber	1 cucumber
½ pint/3 dl. natural yogurt	1¼ cups unflavored yogurt
¼ pint/1½ dl. single cream	⅔ cup coffee cream
1 tablespoon chopped mint	1 tablespoon chopped mint
½ clove garlic	½ clove garlic

Peel and slice the cucumber thinly. Spread the slices on a board and sprinkle with salt. Allow to stand for 30 minutes, then squeeze out the excess moisture. Place the yogurt and cream in a basin and beat well together until smooth. Stir in the cucumber and most of the mint. Rub the cut surface of the garlic over the inside of the individual soup coupes or the soup tureen. Pour in the soup and chill well. Serve sprinkled with the remaining chopped mint.

Eastern beef

Preparation time 15 minutes plus marinating time
Cooking time 20 minutes
Serves 4

IMPERIAL/METRIC	AMERICAN
1½ lb./700 g. beef sirloin	1½ lb. beef sirloin
4 tablespoons castor sugar	⅓ cup sugar
1 tablespoon olive oil	1 tablespoon olive oil
6 tablespoons soy sauce	½ cup soy sauce
1 teaspoon Tabasco sauce	1 teaspoon Tabasco sauce
1 onion	1 onion
2 cloves garlic	2 cloves garlic
1 tablespoon sesame seeds	1 tablespoon sesame seeds
1 tablespoon plain flour	1 tablespoon all-purpose flour
¼ pint/1½ dl. water	⅔ cup water

Cut the meat into thin strips. Mix together the castor sugar, olive oil, soy sauce and Tabasco sauce with a whisk. Chop the onion and garlic finely and add to the previous mixture with the sesame seeds and flour. Pour over the meat and mix well. Cover and leave to marinate for 1 hour.

Turn the mixture into a large saucepan or frying pan, add the water and bring to the boil, stirring. Lower the heat, cover and simmer the mixture for 20 minutes, until the meat is tender. Check the seasoning and serve with rice or noodles.

Blackberry and apple summer gnocchi

Preparation time 15 minutes
Cooking time about 20 minutes
Serves 4–6

IMPERIAL/METRIC	AMERICAN
1 lb./450 g. cooking apples	1 lb. baking apples
8 oz./225 g. blackberries	½ lb. blackberries
sugar to taste	sugar to taste
knob butter	knob butter
3 oz./75 g. fine semolina	½ cup semolina flour
pinch salt	pinch salt
¾ pint/4 dl. milk	2 cups milk
1 oz./25 g. castor sugar	2 tablespoons sugar
1 egg	1 egg
topping	**topping**
2 tablespoons demerara sugar	3 tablespoons brown sugar
1 teaspoon ground cinnamon	1 teaspoon ground cinnamon

Peel, core and slice the apples. Wash the blackberries or use frozen ones. Cook the blackberries and apple, sprinkled with sugar and butter, until tender. Pour into an ovenproof casserole dish.

Make the gnocchi by sprinkling the semolina and salt into the hot milk, stirring, and bring to the boil. Continue cooking for 4 minutes. Remove from the heat and beat in the sugar and egg. Return to the heat for another 2 minutes, then pour into a mould which has been rinsed out with cold water. (Or an 8-inch (20-cm.) square tin or Swiss roll tin.)

When cold, cut into small rounds or squares with a cutter or knife. Arrange overlapping in rows on the hot fruit. Sprinkle the gnocchi with the mixed demerara sugar and cinnamon. Place in a moderately hot oven until the sugar melts and forms a crust. Serve with whipped double cream.

MENU
Smooth liver pâté
Glazed lamb with wine sauce
Malakoff pashka

Smooth liver pâté

Preparation time 15 minutes
Cooking time 1 hour 15 minutes
Serves 6–8

IMPERIAL/METRIC	AMERICAN
6 rashers lean bacon, chopped	6 slices Canadian or other lean bacon, chopped
8 oz./225 g. pig's liver	½ lb. pork liver
6 oz./175 g. chicken livers	⅓ lb. chicken livers
2 cloves garlic	2 cloves garlic
1 egg	1 egg
2 tablespoons cream	3 tablespoons cream
salt and pepper	salt and pepper
3 bay leaves	3 bay leaves

Grease a terrine or straight-sided dish. Mince the bacon, livers and garlic or put into a liquidiser and blend. Add the egg, cream and seasoning and mix well. Turn the mixture into a prepared dish and top with the bay leaves. Cover with foil or a lid. Stand in a roasting tin of hot water and bake in a moderate oven (350°F., 180°C., Gas Mark 4) for 1¼ hours. Allow to become quite cold. Serve with toast.

Note The livers are easier to mince if lightly fried in butter, for half a minute on each side, to firm.

Glazed lamb with wine sauce

Preparation time 10 minutes
Cooking time 1 hour 40 minutes
Serves 4–6

IMPERIAL/METRIC	AMERICAN
1 teaspoon ground bay leaves	1 teaspoon ground bay leaves
1 tablespoon seasoned flour	1 tablespoon seasoned flour
1 small leg or shoulder of lamb	1 small leg or shoulder of lamb
1 clove garlic	1 clove garlic
6 tablespoons red wine	½ cup red wine
2 tablespoons thick honey	3 tablespoons thick honey
4 fresh pears	4 fresh pears
few sprigs watercress	few sprigs watercress
2 oz./50 g. glacé cherries	¼ cup candied cherries
2 teaspoons cornflour	2 teaspoons cornstarch

Mix the ground bay leaves with the seasoned flour. Rub the lamb all over with the cut clove of garlic then the seasoned flour. Place the meat in a roasting tin with the wine and bake in a moderate oven (350°F., 180°C., Gas Mark 4) allowing 25 minutes per 1 lb./½ kg. plus 25 minutes over. After an hour, turn the joint and baste well.

Half an hour before serving, lift out the meat and drain, reserve all the liquid from the roasting tin. Replace the meat, best side up, and spread with honey.

Add the peeled and cored pear halves. Return to the oven and continue cooking, basting the meat and pears once or twice. Serve the meat surrounded with the pears and watercress. Place 2 cherries in each pear half. Make a sauce with the reserved liquid from the roasting tin, ¼ pint (1½ dl., ⅔ cup) water from accompanying vegetables and the cornflour, moistened with a little cold water. Remove any excess fat from the sauce before serving.

Malakoff pashka

Preparation time 10–15 minutes plus draining time
Serves 4–6

IMPERIAL/METRIC	AMERICAN
¼ pint/1½ dl. soured cream	⅔ cup sour cream
2½ oz./65 g. castor sugar	5 tablespoons sugar
8 oz./225 g. cottage cheese, sieved	1 cup sieved cottage cheese
4 oz./100 g. toasted almonds, chopped	1 cup chopped toasted almonds
grated zest of 1 orange	grated zest of 1 orange
2 tablespoons Cointreau or Grand Marnier (or to taste)	3 tablespoons Cointreau or Grand Marnier (or to taste)

Combine the soured cream, sugar and cottage cheese. Add the toasted almonds, orange zest and liqueur, mixing well. Line a small sieve with muslin and fill with the mixture. Leave in a cool place to drain for 24 hours. A weight can be placed on the mixture in the sieve to force out more liquid. When the pashka is firm, remove from the sieve and muslin and serve with sponge fingers.

MENU
Nutty pear starter
Gammon steaks and red cabbage
Cheese board, savoury biscuits, fruit and nuts

Nutty pear starter

Preparation time 15 minutes plus 1 hour chilling time
Serves 4

IMPERIAL/METRIC	AMERICAN
2 oz./50 g. flaked almonds	½ cup flaked or slivered almonds
8 oz./225 g. cream or cottage cheese	1 cup cream or cottage cheese
4 ripe pears	4 ripe pears
juice of 1 lemon	juice of 1 lemon
1 tablespoon white wine	1 tablespoon white wine
2 tablespoons mayonnaise	3 tablespoons mayonnaise
1 tablespoon cream	1 tablespoon cream
dash Tabasco sauce	dash Tabasco sauce
dash Worcestershire sauce	dash Worcestershire sauce
salt and pepper to taste	salt and pepper to taste
1 lettuce	1 lettuce

Chop and toast the almonds. Form the cream or cottage cheese into small balls with the chopped almonds. Chill for 1 hour.

Peel, core and halve the pears, brush liberally with lemon juice to prevent discolouration. Combine the wine, mayonnaise, cream, Tabasco, Worcestershire sauce and seasoning.

Shred the outer leaves of lettuce and place in the centre of a serving dish. Quarter the heart and place on top. Pile the cheese balls on to the pear halves and arrange round the lettuce. Serve this starter with the spicy sauce.

Gammon steaks and red cabbage

Preparation time 15 minutes
Cooking time 30 minutes
Serves 4

IMPERIAL/METRIC	AMERICAN
2 lb./1 kg. red cabbage	2 lb. red cabbage
2 cooking apples	2 baking apples
1 bay leaf	1 bay leaf
3 cloves	3 cloves
2 oz./50 g. sugar	¼ cup sugar
1 oz./25 g. butter	2 tablespoons butter
1–2 tablespoons vinegar	2–3 tablespoons vinegar
4 gammon steaks	4 thick slices uncooked cured ham
4 tablespoons brown sugar	⅓ cup brown sugar
8 cloves	8 cloves

Prepare the cabbage by removing the outer leaves and stalks and shred finely. Peel, core and slice the apples. Put the cabbage into a pan with a little water with the apples, bay leaf, cloves and sugar. Boil for about 25–30 minutes until cooked. Add the butter and vinegar.

Meanwhile, snip the fat, if any, round the gammon steaks and brush with melted butter. Sprinkle with brown sugar and stick with cloves. Put under a high grill then turn down to medium. Turn after about 8 minutes, depending on the thickness of the gammon steak.

MENU
Tuna and crab mousse
Chicken breasts with spicy tomato sauce
Emerald mist mould

Tuna and crab mousse

Preparation time 20 minutes plus setting time
Serves 4

IMPERIAL/METRIC	AMERICAN
aspic jelly crystals	1¼ envelopes gelatin
½ cucumber	½ cucumber
1 (7-oz./200-g.) can tuna	1 (7-oz.) can tuna
1 (1½-oz./40-g.) can crab meat	1 (1½-oz.) can crab meat
¼ pint/1½ dl. mayonnaise	⅔ cup mayonnaise
1 tablespoon tomato purée	1 tablespoon tomato paste
2 drops Tabasco sauce	2 drops Tabasco sauce
¼ pint/1½ dl. double cream	⅔ cup whipping cream
2 egg whites	2 egg whites
salt and pepper to taste	salt and pepper to taste
to garnish	**to garnish**
watercress	watercress
tomatoes	tomatoes

Make up ½ pint (3 dl., 1¼ cups) of aspic jelly according to the instructions on the packet. Pour a little into the bottom of an 8-inch (20-cm.) ring mould and allow to set. Thinly slice the cucumber and arrange on top. Pour over a little more aspic jelly and leave to set again. Flake the tuna into a bowl with the crab meat and add the mayonnaise, tomato purée and Tabasco sauce. Pour the cold aspic jelly into the mixture and stir. Lightly whip the cream, fold into the mixture and leave until thick but not set. Whisk the egg whites stiffly and fold in. Season to taste and turn the mixture into the ring mould. Chill until firm.

Quickly dip the mould into a bowl of hot water and turn out on to a serving dish. Alternatively, this mousse can be served in individual moulds. Garnish with watercress and tomato quarters.

Chicken breasts with spicy tomato sauce

Preparation time 15 minutes
Cooking time 20 minutes
Serves 4

IMPERIAL/METRIC	AMERICAN
4 slices boned chicken breast	4 slices boned chicken breast
2 oz./50 g. butter or margarine	¼ cup butter or margarine
sauce	**sauce**
2 teaspoons brown sugar	2 teaspoons brown sugar
½ teaspoon salt	½ teaspoon salt
4 tablespoons tomato ketchup	⅓ cup tomato catsup
1 teaspoon dry mustard	1 teaspoon dry mustard
2 tablespoons malt vinegar	3 tablespoons malt vinegar
1 small onion, finely chopped	1 small onion, finely chopped

Line a grill pan with aluminium foil. Stir all the sauce ingredients with 1 oz. (25 g.) of the butter, and simmer until a thick consistency is obtained. Brush the chicken breast (to bone chicken breasts, see below) with melted butter and grill for 1 minute on each side. Coat the chicken breast with the sauce, continuing to grill on a low heat for a further 3 minutes, basting frequently. Turn on to the other side and repeat. Serve with salad.

To bone chicken breasts Start with the chicken neck end towards you. Using a sharp filleting knife, carefully remove the breast away from the breastbone, easing the meat with your free hand.

Emerald mist mould

Preparation time 10 minutes plus setting time
Cooking time 10 minutes
Serves 4

IMPERIAL/METRIC	AMERICAN
4 tablespoons cornflour	⅓ cup cornstarch
1 pint/6 dl. milk	2½ cups milk
4 oz./100 g. butter	½ cup butter
3–4 oz./75–100 g. castor sugar	6–8 tablespoons sugar
1 packet lime jelly	1 package lime-flavored gelatin
¾ pint/4 dl. water	2 cups water
3 tablespoons Irish whiskey	¼ cup Irish whiskey

Put the cornflour into a saucepan, blend smoothly with some of the milk. Stir in the rest of the milk and add the butter. Stir over heat until smooth and thick, then cook for 2–3 minutes. Add the sugar to taste and pour into 1 large or 4 individual moulds, rinsed out in cold water. Leave until cold and firm.

Put the jelly into a saucepan with half the water. Stir over the heat until melted, then mix in the rest of the water and the whiskey. Pour into a wide dish to set.

Turn the mould out on to a serving dish. Chop the jelly with a wetted knife, serve it around the mould and decorate the dish with maidenhair fern, if available. The mould can be served without the jelly, in which case it should be flavoured with vanilla or almond essence to taste when the sugar is added.

MENU
Ocean starter
Chicken Veronique
St. Clement's mousse

Ocean starter

Preparation time 10 minutes
Serves 4

IMPERIAL/METRIC	AMERICAN
1 (7-oz./200-g.) can salmon	1 (7-oz.) can salmon
1(7-oz./200-g.) tuna	1 (7-oz.) can tuna
4 oz./100 g. prawns	⅔ cup shrimp or prawns
4 oz./100 g. soft breadcrumbs	2 cups soft bread crumbs
2 tablespoons lemon juice	3 tablespoons lemon juice
4 oz./100 g. butter	½ cup butter
½ teaspoon tarragon	½ teaspoon tarragon
1 tablespoon tomato ketchup	1 tablespoon tomato catsup
1 tablespoon anchovy essence	1 tablespoon anchovy extract
¼ pint/1½ dl. single cream	⅔ cup coffee cream
salt and pepper	salt and pepper
to garnish	**to garnish**
lemon twists	lemon twists
chopped parsley	chopped parsley

Remove any dark skin and bones from the salmon and flake into a bowl, add the tuna with the oil from the can. Chop the prawns roughly and add to the other fish. Mix the fish with the breadcrumbs, add the lemon juice and pour over the melted butter. Add the remaining ingredients and beat well until the mixture is thoroughly mixed. Taste for seasoning then pack into a serving dish, sprinkle the top generously with chopped parsley. Chill well before serving.

Chicken Veronique

Preparation time 15 minutes
Cooking time about 1 hour 30 minutes
Serves 4

IMPERIAL/METRIC	AMERICAN
2 oz./50 g. butter	¼ cup butter
salt and pepper	salt and pepper
tarragon	tarragon
1 (4-lb./2-kg.) chicken	1 (4-lb.) roaster chicken
8 oz./225 g. white grapes	½ lb. green grapes

Place 1 oz. (25 g.) seasoned butter and the tarragon inside the chicken. Smear the remaining butter over the chicken and season with freshly ground black pepper; roast in a hot oven (425°F., 220°C., Gas Mark 7). Reduce the heat after 10 minutes to 375°F., 190°C., Gas Mark 5 and baste occasionally.

Seed the grapes. Liquidise half of them. When the chicken is cooked, carve and place on a heated serving dish. Remove any excess fat from the roasting tin and add the grape purée to the tin. Bring to the boil, stirring, then pour over the chicken. Garnish the dish with the remaining grapes.

St. Clement's mousse

Preparation time 20 minutes
Serves 4

IMPERIAL/METRIC	AMERICAN
1 lemon	1 lemon
1 orange	1 orange
4 tablespoons water	⅓ cup water
½ oz./15 g. gelatine	2 envelopes gelatin
3 large eggs	3 large eggs
4 oz./100 g. castor sugar	½ cup sugar
2 tablespoons hot water	3 tablespoons hot water
to garnish	**to garnish**
lemon and orange slices	lemon and orange slices
sponge finger biscuits	ladyfingers

Grate the rind of the lemon and orange then squeeze the juices. Put the 4 tablespoons water in a small saucepan and sprinkle with the gelatine. Heat gently until the gelatine dissolves. Leave to cool.

Separate the eggs into 2 bowls. Add 3 oz. (75 g./ 6 tablespoons) of the sugar and the hot water to the yolks and whisk until the mixture is thick and fluffy. Next add the rind and juice, whisking well to mix, and finally pour in the gelatine stirring well. Leave aside until cold, stirring occasionally, until mixture begins to stiffen. Add the remaining sugar and whisk until the mixture is glossy. Beat the egg whites until very stiff and fold into the orange and lemon mixture, using a metal spoon or rubber spatula, until it is evenly mixed. Pour into individual glasses and decorate with lemon and orange slices and finger biscuits. Serve slightly chilled.

MENU
Festive avocados
Cod Acapulco
Sunset pears

Festive avocados

Preparation time 10 minutes
Serves 4

IMPERIAL/METRIC	AMERICAN
2 ripe avocado pears	2 ripe avocados
juice of 1 orange	juice of 1 orange
8 oz./225 g. cooked chicken or turkey, diced	1 cup diced cooked chicken or turkey
2 tablespoons chopped pimento	3 tablespoons chopped pimiento
1 tablespoon tomato juice or mayonnaise	1 tablespoon tomato juice or mayonnaise
1 tablespoon Worcestershire sauce	1 tablespoon Worcestershire sauce
1 teaspoon salt	1 teaspoon salt
good pinch paprika pepper	good pinch paprika pepper
watercress	watercress
to garnish	**to garnish**
pimento	pimiento
green pepper	green sweet pepper

Wash and polish the avocados, cut in half lengthways and remove the stones. Brush the insides with orange juice. Combine the chicken or turkey, chopped pimento, tomato juice, Worcestershire sauce and seasoning. Blend thoroughly to a fairly stiff mixture. Fill the avocado halves with the chicken or turkey mixture. Garnish with very thin slices of pimento and a 'V' of green pepper.

Serve very cold on a bed of watercress and garnish this with some additional pimento.

Cod Acapulco

Preparation time 10–15 minutes plus marinating time
Cooking time 30 minutes
Serves 4

Cut the cod into 1–2-inch (2·5–5-cm.) pieces. Mix the cod with the lime juice and leave to marinate for about 4 hours, stirring occasionally. Heat the olive oil in a saucepan and gently fry the onion until tender but not brown. Add the tomatoes, tomato juice, thyme, salt and Tabasco sauce. Bring to the boil. Place the marinated cod in an ovenproof casserole dish, pour the tomato mixture over. Cover and cook in a moderately hot oven (400°F., 200°C., Gas Mark 6) for 20–30 minutes, or until the fish is tender. Serve sprinkled with chopped parsley.

IMPERIAL/METRIC	AMERICAN
2 lb./1 kg. cod fillet	2 lb. cod fillet
¼ pint/1½ dl. lime juice cordial	⅔ cup undiluted lime drink
2 tablespoons olive oil	3 tablespoons olive oil
2 medium onions, finely chopped	2 medium onions, finely chopped
3 tomatoes, skinned and coarsely chopped	3 tomatoes, skinned and coarsely chopped
¼ pint/1½ dl. tomato juice	⅔ cup tomato juice
pinch dried thyme	pinch dried thyme
salt	salt
few drops Tabasco sauce	few drops Tabasco sauce
to garnish	**to garnish**
chopped parsley	chopped parsley

Sunset pears

Preparation time 15 minutes
Cooking time 20–25 minutes
Serves 4

IMPERIAL/METRIC	AMERICAN
1 tablespoon cornflour	1 tablespoon cornstarch
¼ pint/1½ dl. orange juice	⅔ cup orange juice
2 tablespoons lemon juice	3 tablespoons lemon juice
1 tablespoon sweet sherry or Madeira	1 tablespoon sweet sherry or Madeira
2 tablespoons brown sugar	3 tablespoons brown sugar
2 oz./50 g. castor sugar	¼ cup sugar
pinch salt	pinch salt
1 tablespoon orange rind	1 tablespoon orange rind
1 oz./25 g. butter	2 tablespoons butter
8 ripe pears	8 ripe pears
8 cloves	8 cloves

Blend the cornflour with a little orange juice then add the remaining ingredients except the pears and cloves. Cook over a low heat stirring all the time until the mixture thickens. Peel the pears and place in a lightly buttered ovenproof dish. Stick a clove in the top of each pear and pour the syrup over the pears. Bake in a moderate oven (350°F., 180°C., Gas Mark 4) for 20–25 minutes. Serve with whipped cream.

MENU
Savoury melon coupe
Pineapple chicken drumsticks
Coffee ice cream with maple syrup sauce

Savoury melon coupe

Preparation time 15 minutes plus 30 minutes
marinating time
Serves 4

IMPERIAL/METRIC	AMERICAN
1 medium melon	1 medium melon
4 oz./100 g. prawns	⅔ cup shrimp
dressing	**dressing**
¼ teaspoon ginger	¼ teaspoon ginger
pinch salt	pinch salt
pinch sugar	pinch sugar
pinch pepper	pinch pepper
¼ teaspoon French mustard	¼ teaspoon French mustard
2 tablespoons wine vinegar	3 tablespoons wine vinegar
4 tablespoons oil	⅓ cup oil
to garnish	**to garnish**
cucumber slices	cucumber slices

Slice the top off the melon and remove the seeds. Scoop out the flesh from the melon using a ball cutter, or remove large pieces and cut into cubes.

Mix the seasonings for the dressing with the wine vinegar and oil. Marinate the prawns in the dressing for at least 30 minutes, then mix with the melon balls. Vandyke the edge of the melon shell with kitchen scissors. Place the melon ball mixture into the melon shell. Chill until ready to serve. Garnish.

Pineapple chicken drumsticks

Preparation time 30 minutes
Cooking time 45 minutes
Serves 4

IMPERIAL/METRIC	AMERICAN
4 large chicken drumsticks	4 large chicken drumsticks
salt and pepper	salt and pepper
4 canned pineapple spears	4 canned pineapple spears
4 slices cooked ham	4 slices cooked cured ham
2 oz./50 g. butter	¼ cup butter
¼ pint/1½ dl. chicken stock	⅔ cup chicken stock
1 bay leaf	1 bay leaf
½ teaspoon dried mixed herbs	½ teaspoon dried mixed herbs
½ teaspoon curry powder	½ teaspoon curry powder
2 oz./50 g. flour	½ cup all-purpose flour
½ pint/3 dl. milk	1¼ cups milk
2 tablespoons double cream	3 tablespoons cream

Bone the drumsticks by cutting round at the knuckle end with a sharp knife, then pull the meat away from the bone. Next cut away from the bone at the joint and lay the boned drumstick flat, season with salt and pepper. Place a pineapple spear on each slice of ham and roll up. Insert the ham rolls in the drumsticks and secure together firmly with wooden cocktail sticks. Melt a little of the butter in a frying pan and fry the drumsticks until golden brown. Transfer the chicken to a casserole and add the chicken stock, bay leaf and herbs. Cover and cook in the moderately hot oven (400°F., 200°C., Gas Mark 6) for 30 minutes.

Meanwhile, in the pan used for the chicken, melt the remaining butter and add the curry powder and the flour, stir to make a roux. Add the milk, salt and pepper and eventually strain the juice from the chicken. Stir well over a low heat and finally add the cream. Pour the sauce over the chicken and return to the oven to reheat. Serve with peas and potatoes.

Coffee ice cream with maple syrup sauce

Preparation time 10–15 minutes plus freezing time
Cooking time about 5 minutes for sauce
Serves 4

IMPERIAL/METRIC	AMERICAN
2 eggs, separated	2 eggs, separated
4 tablespoons icing sugar	5 tablespoons confectioners' sugar
2 tablespoons coffee essence	3 tablespoons coffee extract
1 tablespoon brandy (optional)	1 tablespoon brandy (optional)
¼ pint/1½ dl. double cream	⅔ cup heavy cream
maple syrup sauce	**maple syrup sauce**
scant ½ pint/¼ litre maple syrup	1 cup maple syrup
2 tablespoons water	3 tablespoons water
½ oz./15 g. butter	1 tablespoon butter
grated rind and juice of 1 orange	grated rind and juice of 1 orange

Whisk the egg whites until stiff and fold in the sieved icing sugar. Mix the egg yolks, coffee essence and brandy if used, then fold into the egg whites. Whip the cream lightly and fold into the egg mixture. Pour into a 1-lb. (½-kg.) loaf tin. Place in a freezer or freezing compartment of a refrigerator until set. Scoop out and serve with the maple syrup sauce.

For the sauce, place all the ingredients in a heavy-based saucepan. Simmer gently for 3–4 minutes.

MENU
Aspic castles
Veal cutlets suprême
Tropical fruit salad (canned)

Aspic castles

Preparation time about 30 minutes
Serves 4

IMPERIAL/METRIC	AMERICAN
6 tablespoons frozen mixed vegetables	½ cup frozen mixed vegetables
1 bunch radishes	1 bunch radishes
1 chicken stock cube	1 chicken bouillon cube
1 tablespoon aspic jelly crystals	1 tablespoon gelatin
1 tablespoon dry sherry	1 tablespoon dry sherry
4 oz./100 g. cooked chicken or turkey, diced	½ cup diced cooked chicken or turkey
3 tablespoons cooked rice	¼ cup cooked rice
salt and pepper	salt and pepper
1 egg, hard-boiled	1 egg, hard-cooked
1 small lettuce, shredded	1 small lettuce, shredded

Thaw the vegetables, blanch in boiling water for 3 minutes and drain well. Top and tail the radishes, slice 8 thinly and add to the vegetables. From the remaining radishes, make radish roses by cutting each radish across from the tip down to within a ¼ inch (0·5 cm.) from the base. Repeat 3 times. Leave the radishes in cold water for half an hour to open out. Pour ¾ pint (4 dl., 2 cups) boiling water over the stock cube and add the jelly crystals. Stir until dissolved and allow to cool. Add the sherry.

Rinse out 8 small coffee cups or dariole moulds with cold water. When the aspic is syrupy and beginning to set, pour 1 tablespoon into each mould. Stir the vegetables, diced chicken and rice into the rest of the aspic jelly, season and as soon as the first jelly layer is set, spoon in most of the jelly mixture. Chill until set. Finish with a slice of hard-boiled egg and remaining aspic.

To serve, wring out a tea towel in very hot water and press round each mould or cup and turn out on to a bed of shredded lettuce. Garnish with radish roses.

Veal cutlets suprême

Preparation time 5 minutes
Cooking time 20 minutes
Serves 4

IMPERIAL/METRIC	AMERICAN
4 veal cutlets, boned	4 veal cutlets, boned
salt and pepper	salt and pepper
2 oz./50 g. butter	¼ cup butter
pinch mace	pinch mace
3 tablespoons sherry	¼ cup sherry
½ pint/3 dl. double cream	1¼ cups heavy cream
1 oz./25 g. cheese, grated	¼ cup grated cheese
to garnish	**to garnish**
pimento strips	pimiento strips
sprigs parsley	sprigs parsley

Season the veal cutlets with salt and pepper. Melt the butter in a frying pan and fry the cutlets until golden brown on both sides. Remove and keep warm in a flameproof serving dish.

Add the mace and sherry to the frying pan and cook gently for a few minutes. Pour in the cream and cook over a low heat for a few minutes. Pour over the cutlets, sprinkle with the cheese and grill lightly. Garnish with strips of pimento and sprigs of parsley. Serve with sauté potatoes and green salad.

MENU
Watercress soup
Scallops in piquant tomato sauce
Chicken and ham en croûte
Tipsy fruit salad (see page 105)

Watercress soup

Preparation time 10 minutes
Cooking time 30 minutes
Serves 4

IMPERIAL/METRIC	AMERICAN
2 large bunches watercress	2 large bunches watercress
1 oz./25 g. butter	2 tablespoons butter
3 spring onions	3 scallions
1 pint/6 dl. chicken stock	2½ cups chicken stock
¼ pint/1½ dl. natural yogurt	⅔ cup unflavored yogurt
2 egg yolks	2 egg yolks
salt and pepper	salt and pepper
to garnish	**to garnish**
chopped chives	chopped chives
watercress	watercress

Wash the watercress and chop finely. Melt the butter in a saucepan and cook the chopped spring onions until they are soft but not brown. Add the watercress and stock and bring to the boil. Cover and simmer for about 20 minutes. Blend the mixture in a liquidiser or rub through a sieve. Mix the yogurt and egg yolks together and add gradually to the soup. Season and reheat gently but do not allow to boil. Sprinkle with fresh chopped chives and add a sprig of watercress to the centre of each bowl of soup.

Scallops in piquant tomato sauce

Preparation time 15 minutes
Cooking time 20 minutes
Serves 4–6

IMPERIAL/METRIC	AMERICAN
4–6 scallops	4–6 scallops
4 tablespoons dry white wine	⅓ cup dry white wine
2 tablespoons water	3 tablespoons water
1 bay leaf	1 bay leaf
freshly ground black pepper	freshly ground black pepper
1 recipe piquant tomato sauce (see page 26)	1 recipe piquant tomato sauce (see page 26)
to garnish	**to garnish**
chopped parsley	chopped parsley

Wash the scallops and chop in half. Heat the wine and water with the bay leaf and pepper in a small saucepan and poach the scallops for 4–5 minutes. Add the scallops to the piquant tomato sauce and cook for a few minutes. Meanwhile, reduce the poaching liquid by half and add to the tomato sauce.

Serve in heated ramekin dishes or heated scallop shells and sprinkle with chopped parsley.

Chicken and ham en croûte

Preparation time 30 minutes
Cooking time 2 hours
Serves 4

IMPERIAL/METRIC	AMERICAN
2 oz./50 g. butter	¼ cup butter
1 large onion	1 large onion
4 oz./100 g. mushrooms	1 cup mushrooms
salt and pepper	salt and pepper
8 oz./225 g. poached chicken breasts, chopped	1 cup chopped poached chicken breasts
1-lb./450-g. cooked joint bacon or ham	1-lb. cooked cured ham or bacon joint
1 egg yolk mixed with water	1 egg yolk mixed with water
pastry	**pastry**
12 oz./350 g. plain flour	3 cups all-purpose flour
pinch salt	pinch salt
4 oz./100 g. lard	½ cup lard
¼ pint/1½ dl. water plus 2 tablespoons	⅔ cup water plus 2 tablespoons
to garnish	**to garnish**
frosted grapes	frosted grapes

Melt the butter and fry the chopped onion for 5 minutes. Add the mushrooms. Fry for a further 5 minutes. Season to taste.

Sieve the flour and salt into a basin. Put the lard and water into a saucepan and bring to boil. Pour on to the flour and mix with a knife until it forms a ball. Roll the pastry out to a circle, reserving a little. Spread the circle with the onion mixture. Place a layer of chicken in the centre. Cover with the ham joint and remaining chicken. Brush the edges of the pastry with beaten egg and completely enclose the meat. Seal the edges well and place on a baking tray. Decorate with pastry leaves and balls made from the reserved pastry. Brush with beaten egg and bake in a hot oven (425°F., 210°C., Gas Mark 7) for 15 minutes. Lower the heat and bake for 1½ hours. If the pastry becomes too brown, cover with greaseproof paper. Serve with frosted grapes.

To make frosted grapes, brush small bunches of grapes with beaten egg white. Toss in castor sugar and leave to dry on greaseproof paper.

MENU
Tipsy grapefruit
Cod's roe pâté
Pork in sour cream sauce
Lemon dream cake with chocolate ice cream

Tipsy grapefruit

Preparation time 10 minutes plus 1 hour standing time
Cooking time about 2 minutes
Serves 4

IMPERIAL/METRIC	AMERICAN
2 grapefruit	2 grapefruit
2 tablespoons brown sugar	3 tablespoons brown sugar
4 teaspoons rum	4 teaspoons rum
ground ginger	ground ginger

Cut the grapefruit in half and carefully loosen the segments, taking out the white membranes where possible. Sprinkle with the sugar and rum and allow to stand at room temperature for about an hour. When required to serve, place under a hot grill for 1–2 minutes, until the tops are golden and bubbling. Dust the grapefruit halves with ground ginger before serving.

Cod's roe pâté

Preparation time 10 minutes
Serves 4

IMPERIAL/METRIC	AMERICAN
8 oz./225 g. cod's roe	½ lb. cod's roe
4 tablespoons oil	⅓ cup oil
1½ tablespoons lemon juice	2 tablespoons lemon juice
freshly ground black pepper	freshly ground black pepper
2 tablespoons chopped parsley	3 tablespoons chopped parsley

Beat the cod's roe with half the oil until a creamy mixture is obtained. Allow the mixture time to rest for a few minutes in the refrigerator, then gradually beat in the remaining ingredients, alternating lemon juice and oil until a creamy mixture is obtained. Alternatively, make the pâté in a liquidiser adding the oil gradually to the cod's roe using the same method as for mayonnaise.

Pork in sour cream sauce

Preparation time 10 minutes
Cooking time 15 minutes
Serves 4

IMPERIAL/METRIC	AMERICAN
4 pieces pork fillet or veal escalopes	4 pieces pork fillet or veal scallops
1 oz./25 g. flour	¼ cup all-purpose flour
salt and pepper	salt and pepper
2 oz./50 g. butter	¼ cup butter
4 oz./100 g. mushrooms, thinly sliced	1 cup thinly sliced mushrooms
¼ pint/1½ dl. soured cream	⅔ cup sour cream

Beat out the pork fillet or veal until thin and coat in flour, seasoned with salt and pepper. Fry in the butter for about 5 minutes on each side or until cooked. Place on a serving dish and keep warm.

Add the mushrooms to the butter in the pan and fry for 3–4 minutes or until cooked. Stir in any remaining flour and cook for a minute. Remove from the heat and stir in the cream. Reheat very gently until piping hot. *Do not allow to boil.* Season to taste and pour over the pork. Garnish with piles of heated carrots, sprinkled with chives.

Lemon dream cake

Preparation time 30 minutes
Cooking time 30–35 minutes

IMPERIAL/METRIC	AMERICAN
4 oz./100 g. butter	½ cup butter
4 oz./100 g. castor sugar	½ cup sugar
grated rind of 1 lemon	grated rind of 1 lemon
2 eggs	2 eggs
2 tablespoons drinking chocolate	3 tablespoons sweetened cocoa powder
4 oz./100 g. self-raising flour	1 cup all-purpose flour sifted with 2 teaspoons baking powder
1 teaspoon baking powder	
2 tablespoons milk	3 tablespoons milk
1 oz./25 g. peanuts	1 tablespoon peanuts
3 oz./75 g. chocolate	3 oz. chocolate
to decorate	**to decorate**
4 oz./100 g. butter	½ cup butter
6–8 oz./175–225 g. icing sugar, sieved	1⅓–1¾ cups sifted confectioners' sugar
juice of 1 lemon	juice of 1 lemon
yellow 'mimosa balls'	yellow cake decorations
filling	**filling**
4 oz./100 g. lemon curd	⅓ cup lemon custard filling

Cream the butter and sugar until light and fluffy, add the lemon rind then beat in the eggs one at a time. Fold in the sieved dry ingredients alternately with the milk. Finally fold in the chopped peanuts and chopped chocolate. Divide the mixture between 2 6-inch (15-cm.) greased cake tins lined with grease-proof paper and bake in a moderate oven (350°F., 180°C., Gas Mark 4) for 30–35 minutes.

Beat the butter for the decoration until soft and creamy. Add the sieved icing sugar a little at a time, beating well after each addition. Add the juice from the lemon before all the sugar has been incorporated. Put the layers together, filling the centre with the lemon curd. Coat the sides and top with the butter cream and decorate with a cake ruler.

Stiffen the remainder of the cream with a little icing sugar and pipe rosettes, using an 8-star tube, round the top of the cake. Decorate with yellow 'mimosa balls'. If liked, serve with bought chocolate ice cream.

MENU
Fondue bourguignonne
Pepper and onion relish, Mustard sauce, Béarnaise sauce, Curry sauce, Tomato relish, Corn relish and green salad

Fondue bourguignonne

ILLUSTRATED IN COLOUR ON PAGE 75
Preparation time 10 minutes
Serves 4

IMPERIAL/METRIC	AMERICAN
1½ lb./700 g. fillet or rump steak	1½ lb. filet or rump steak
vegetable oil for frying	vegetable oil for frying

Cut the meat into 1-inch (2·5-cm.) cubes. Heat the oil in the fondue dish. When a cube of bread browns quickly and floats to the surface, the oil is the correct temperature for cooking the steak. Each guest selects a fondue fork – if the handles are all different colours it makes it easier to recognise ones own fork. Spear a cube of meat firmly on the fork, plunge into the dish and leave propped against the side until the meat is cooked to taste – 1–2 minutes. Dip the cooked meat in one of the following sauces. Remember to try them all in turn. Serve with a crisp green salad.

Pepper and onion relish

Preparation time 15 minutes

Chop the peppers, onion and cucumber into small dice. Melt the sugar in the water, add the vinegar and boil the diced vegetables until soft but not mushy.

IMPERIAL/METRIC	AMERICAN
2 green peppers	2 green sweet peppers
1 onion	1 onion
½ cucumber	½ cucumber
2 tablespoons sugar	3 tablespoons sugar
2 tablespoons water	3 tablespoons water
¼ pint/1½ dl. vinegar	⅔ cup vinegar

Mustard sauce

Preparation time 5 minutes

Mix the mustard and cream together, season well.

IMPERIAL/METRIC	AMERICAN
2 tablespoons French mustard	3 tablespoons French mustard
¼ pint/1½ dl. soured cream	⅔ cup sour cream
salt and pepper to taste	salt and pepper to taste

Béarnaise sauce

Preparation time 10–15 minutes

Whisk the vinegar, egg yolks and seasoning over hot water. Add the chopped butter, whisking while the butter is melting. Chop the gherkins and add to the sauce before serving.

IMPERIAL/METRIC	AMERICAN
1 teaspoon wine vinegar	1 teaspoon wine vinegar
2 egg yolks	2 egg yolks
salt and pepper to taste	salt and pepper to taste
4 oz./100 g. butter	½ cup butter
chopped gherkins	chopped sweet dill pickles

Curry sauce

Preparation time about 25 minutes

Peel and chop the apple and onion. Heat the oil in a saucepan and fry the apple and onion until pale brown. Sprinkle with the curry powder and flour. Stir into the mixture well then add the carrot and stock or water. Lastly sprinkle the sultanas into the mixture and season with salt. Bring to the boil and simmer until the sauce is thick. Add the mango chutney and mix well before serving.

IMPERIAL/METRIC	AMERICAN
1 large cooking apple	1 large baking apple
1 large onion	1 large onion
1 tablespoon oil	1 tablespoon oil
2 teaspoons curry powder	2 teaspoons curry powder
1 teaspoon flour	1 teaspoon flour
1 carrot, grated	1 carrot, grated
½ pint/3 dl. stock or water	1¼ cups stock or water
1 tablespoon sultanas	1 tablespoon seedless white raisins
pinch salt	pinch salt
1 tablespoon mango chutney	1 tablespoon mango chutney

Tomato relish

Preparation time 5 minutes

Mix the garlic, tomato purée, sugar and paprika pepper together. Fold this mixture into the mayonnaise.

IMPERIAL/METRIC	AMERICAN
1 clove garlic, crushed	1 clove garlic, crushed
2 tablespoons tomato purée	3 tablespoons tomato paste
½ teaspoon sugar	½ teaspoon sugar
½ teaspoon paprika pepper	½ teaspoon paprika pepper
6 tablespoons mayonnaise	½ cup mayonnaise

Corn relish – can be purchased from most large supermarkets.

Hot buffet supper

MENU

Mushroom and pepper barquettes
Buffet style chicken in red wine
Saffron rice
Chocolate almond gâteau
Pineapple shells
French cheese selection with biscuits and butter

Mushroom and pepper barquettes

Preparation time 20 minutes
Cooking time 15 minutes
Makes about 30

IMPERIAL/METRIC	AMERICAN
4 eggs	4 eggs
salt and black pepper	salt and black pepper
4 tablespoons single cream	⅓ cup coffee cream
1½ oz./40 g. butter	3 tablespoons butter
2 oz./50 g. mushrooms	½ cup mushrooms
¼ green pepper, blanched	¼ green pepper, blanched
¼ red pepper, blanched	¼ red sweet pepper, blanched
8 oz./225 g. cheese pastry using 8 oz. (225 g.) flour etc.	½ lb. cheese paste using 2 cups all-purpose flour etc.

Whisk the eggs together with the seasoning and cream. Melt 1 oz. (25 g.) of the butter in a saucepan and pour in the eggs. Cook over a low heat, stirring all the time, until the eggs are cooked, but not dry. Chop the mushrooms and pepper and sauté in the remaining butter for 1 minute. Drain and stir into the scrambled egg, allow to cool.

Roll out the pastry and line 30 boat tins. Prick the bases and bake in a preheated moderately hot oven (400°F., 200°C., Gas Mark 6) for 10–15 minutes.

Fill each case with the scrambled egg mixture.

Buffet style chicken in red wine

Preparation time 25 minutes
Cooking time about 50 minutes
Serves 8–10

IMPERIAL/METRIC	AMERICAN
4 rashers streaky bacon	4 bacon slices
3 oz./75 g. butter	6 tablespoons butter
1 onion	1 onion
1 clove garlic	1 clove garlic
8–10 chicken drumsticks	8–10 chicken drumsticks
1 tablespoon brandy	1 tablespoon brandy
sprig of rosemary	sprig of rosemary
bay leaf	bay leaf
sprig of thyme	sprig of thyme
½ pint/3 dl. chicken stock	1¼ cups chicken stock
salt and pepper	salt and pepper
¼ pint/1½ dl. red wine	⅔ cup red wine
20 button onions	20 tiny onions
30 button mushrooms	30 button mushrooms
2 oz./50 g. flour	½ cup all-purpose flour

Fry the rashers of bacon in a frying pan with about a third of the butter. Add the quartered onion and the crushed clove of garlic. When all the fat has come out of the bacon, remove to a casserole with the onion. Fry the drumsticks in the fat until golden brown. Heat the brandy in a ladle, set alight and pour it over the chicken. Remove the chicken to the casserole. Add the herbs, stock, seasoning and wine and put the covered dish in oven (350°F., 180°C., Gas Mark 4).

While the chicken is cooking, fry the onions and mushrooms gently in the fat until golden brown. Add to the chicken and allow the whole dish to cook for 35 minutes. Serve the chicken drumsticks arranged on a heated serving dish with the onions and mushrooms. Pour the sauce into a saucepan and allow to boil rapidly until it is reduced. Rub the flour and remaining butter together. Remove the quartered onion and herbs from the sauce and stir in the butter and flour until the sauce is thickened. Taste for seasoning then pour over the chicken pieces or serve separately. Garnish with parsley and watercress.

Saffron rice

Preparation time 5 minutes
Cooking time 20 minutes
Serves 8

IMPERIAL/METRIC	AMERICAN
1 oz./25 g. butter	2 tablespoons butter
1 small onion, finely chopped	1 small onion, finely chopped
1 lb./450 g. long grain rice	1 lb. long grain rice
1¼ pints/7½ dl. chicken stock	3 cups chicken stock
salt and pepper	salt and pepper
¼ teaspoon saffron	¼ teaspoon saffron

Melt the butter in a fireproof casserole. Sauté the onion gently in the butter. Add the uncooked rice and stir until the grains are coated with butter. Add the stock, seasoning and saffron. Cover the casserole and simmer on top of the cooker for about 20 minutes, until the rice is tender.

Chocolate almond gâteau

Preparation time 25 minutes
Cooking time 25–30 minutes

IMPERIAL/METRIC	AMERICAN
6 eggs	6 eggs
8 oz./225 g. castor sugar	1 cup sugar
6 oz./175 g. self-raising flour	1½ cups all-purpose flour sifted with 1½ teaspoons baking powder
pinch salt	pinch salt
2 tablespoons hot water	3 tablespoons hot water
2 oz./50 g. butter or margarine, melted	¼ cup melted butter or margarine
icing	**icing**
2–3 tablespoons cocoa powder	3–4 tablespoons unsweetened cocoa powder
4 tablespoons hot water	⅓ cup hot water
4 oz./100 g. butter	½ cup butter
10 oz./275 g. icing sugar, sieved	2¼ cups sifted confectioners' sugar
1 tablespoon milk	1 tablespoon milk
to decorate	**to decorate**
flaked almonds, toasted	flaked almonds, toasted

Preheat the oven to moderately hot (400°C., 200°F., Gas Mark 6). Separate the eggs carefully. Beat the whites until stiff, then gradually add the castor sugar and continue beating as for meringues. Add the egg yolks, beating all the time. Sieve the flour and salt and fold in with a metal spoon. Add the hot water and butter by pouring down the side of the bowl and then fold in until combined with the egg mixture. Pour into a greased and floured 8-inch (20-cm.) tin and place in the preheated oven for 15 minutes then lower the heat to moderate (350°F., 180°C., Gas Mark 4) for a further 10–15 minutes. Turn out and cool.

Cut the cooled cake into three layers. To make the butter icing, blend the cocoa powder with the hot water and leave to cool. Beat the butter until softened, then mix in the icing sugar, milk and blended cocoa powder to form a fairly soft icing. Use some of the icing to sandwich the cakes together. With a palette knife, smooth a little of the remaining icing round the sides; roll the coated sides in toasted flaked almonds. Place the cake on a serving plate and smooth most of the remaining icing over the surface and pipe a border of stars round the top edge of the icing. Decorate with almonds as shown on the jacket.

Pineapple shells

Preparation time 15 minutes
Serves 8

IMPERIAL/METRIC	AMERICAN
2 medium pineapples	2 medium pineapples
1½ lb./700 g. mixed fresh fruits e.g. grapes, diced bananas, orange segments, raspberries, diced apple etc.	1½ lb. mixed fresh fruits e.g. grapes, diced bananas, orange segments, raspberries, diced apple etc.
2 tablespoons desiccated coconut	3 tablespoons shredded coconut
8 fl. oz./2½ dl. ginger ale or fruit juice	1 cup ginger ale or fruit juice
3 tablespoons Kirsch	4 tablespoons Kirsch

Cut the pineapples in half. Remove the flesh and dice. Mix with a selection of prepared fruit and coconut. Pour over the ginger ale or fruit juice and Kirsch. Replace the fruit in the pineapple halves. Chill and serve.

Party table settings

An attractively set table makes appetising food even better. Be creative in planning unusual and harmonious effects. You need not be limited by the colour or style of your 'best' china to one stereotyped table setting. For instance, a simple pale blue service might be laid on bare polished wood, bottle green linen, dazzling white damask, or a strongly-patterned cloth, ranging from pale coffee through orange to dark tobacco browns. The choice of table mats, candles and flowers can contrast with or complement the colour of the china, making endless different effects possible. Silverware and silver condiment sets give an entirely different effect from stainless steel, or wooden-handled cutlery, wooden salt and pepper shakers, and salad bowls.

Develop an eye for balanced colour contrast and proportions. A colour wheel shows the complete spectrum, in which complementary colours, giving a complete contrast, fall opposite, for instance cherry red and navy blue. Adjacent colours which clash pleasantly such as jade green and turquoise blue also combine effectively.

A small over-crowded table with an over-powering centrepiece looks just as uninviting as a large sparsely-set table with a tiny posy of flowers in the middle. If the table is rather large, a shallow tray or basket of generous size filled with ornamental fruits and vegetables, including a few gourds, would be better proportioned. A plain tablecloth makes the most of a small table and patterned mats on polished wood break up the empty expanse of a really large table.

Even the height of candles is important; long-stemmed glasses seem to balance tall candles better than short ones. In an assymetric shallow flower arrangement, two candles could be placed at differing heights, off-centre in the container. For a setting which seems to lack interest, champagne coupes or sundae glasses are decorative massed with small tightly-packed flowers, each glass with a candle in

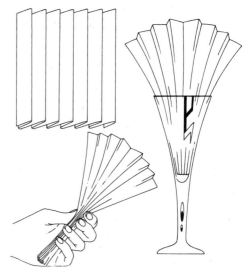

Fold a large stiffened napkin in half and then into inch-wide concertina folds. Holding the bottom, press the napkin into a wine glass so the top fans out attractively.

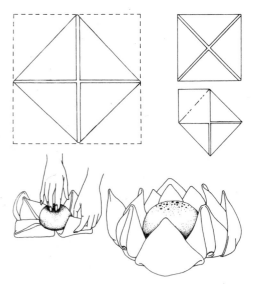

Take a large stiffened, square napkin and fold the four corners to the centre, pressing down well. Repeat this twice more.

Turn the napkin over, holding the points in position, fold the four points once to the centre on the other side. Take a small tumbler, place in the centre and pull up the points carefully from underneath. When all twelve points have been pulled up, the napkin will be transformed into a waterlily. Place a bread roll in the centre for the finishing touch.

the centre, and placed at the right or left hand of individual settings. They must stand firmly on their bases, to avoid any danger of being knocked over. Posy ring bowls can have candles grouped in the centre or placed at regular intervals among the flowers.

Rules for the placing of cutlery at luncheon or dinner are not so rigid as they were. A small knife is often put ready on a side plate, on the fork side, perhaps over a folded napkin. An elegant slim shape is made by folding the napkin in half, then in three, concertina fashion. The knife is used for bread, butter, and finally cheese throughout the meal. Another choice, the waterlily, is easy to achieve as shown in the drawing. A new idea is to fold the napkin in inch-wide map folds, holding the bottom neatly pleated and pressing the centre down into a wine glass so the top fans out prettily (see drawing). Light spray starch on linen napkins before ironing makes fancy folding easy.

Other cutlery is laid working inwards from the first item to be used (unless it is a small spoon or fork which comes on the plate with the meal starter). The inside items will be a dessert fork and spoon, or these may be laid across the top of the setting. A large mat which is heatproof and holds all the cutlery looks well on polished wood, and usually has a matching tiny mat for glasses. Forks should be on the left, knives and spoons on the right, with knife blades facing inwards. Glasses range from above the bowl of the dessertspoon, to above the knife point, outwards, in the order of drinking. (Usually serve white or rosé wine first, then red; if there are more courses, sherry first, rosé or red with the main course, and a sweet white wine with the dessert.) At lunchtime, a coffee tray is usually set ready on a side table, with mats for the main dishes to be served away from the table. Or the main course may come to the table ready served on plates. Since large tables are less common, the main dish and vegetables are usually served from the side table, not placed on the dining table for the host to carve and the hostess to ladle out vegetables, while the guests hand round gravy or sauce. But this charming old custom is now reviving and, providing the serving dishes are really hot, and warm covers are put over the vegetables, this provides a pleasant excuse to offer second portions. The food not being left on the table is usually a polite hint that empty plates will be cleared away at once for the next course to begin.

Formal and informal buffets

Limited kitchen space and seating accommodation make it almost a necessity to entertain large numbers buffet style. Here the arrangement of the serving table is all-important, because all the guests want to approach the table and serve themselves simultaneously.

Formal – table set against the wall Prevent awkward collisions by arranging the items in the order they will be collected, and so that guests can start from both ends if at all possible. At the back of the table at one end you may have an impressive facing flower arrangement, and at the other fresh fruit piled up on a stand. Or at either end a matching pair of candelabra or those beautifully simple teak candlesticks. The centrepiece might be a superb cheese board with baskets of bread piled high behind, butter to the fore and paper napkins as the finishing touch. If the choice includes hot and cold food, I would place cold sweets on one side of the cheese and hot ones on the other, with piles of small plates or dishes in front, and a display of dessert cutlery. A plate warmer at one end can accommodate soup tureens, covered casseroles, hot vegetables, all with the necessary cutlery and plates in piles at the front. Starting from the other end, provide assorted cold cuts of meat and poultry, and a variety of salads. This method leaves space for guests to seat themselves, out of doors or in another room, at small round tables, and if so, all the cutlery, napkins and glasses can be laid on these tables. Duplicate dishes can be substituted for empty ones as this becomes necessary.

Informal – table set away from wall For a party where guests will stand about eating, service is much easier if the traffic round the table can flow from one end round both sides. Remember, the food must all be planned to be eaten with a fork or the fingers and a side table provided to accommodate the used plates and utensils, which should be unobtrusively yet frequently cleared. Guests can then arm themselves with more cutlery for the sweet or cheese course. Drinks are very much better served by one person who is in charge, from a separate trolley or table. If space is really at a premium, a large table can be pushed against one wall and guests will have to take their turn in serving themselves. If the table stands away from the wall, a centrepiece of fruit which can be eaten is better than a flower arrangement. Grapes are particularly eye-catching and delicious. Small bunches can be frosted with sugar for the purpose.

Colourful dishes for special occasions

Most families enjoy a special dish to celebrate a red letter day in the calendar, especially if guests are expected.

Simple pancakes, sprinkled with lemon juice and sugar, are a 'must' on Shrove Tuesday for instance. If you have a heart-shaped cake tin, any favourite sponge mixture can be baked in it and then decorated. This is suitable for St. Valentine's day or to celebrate an engagement. For a wedding buffet, a large one-tier square wedding cake is ideal because it is relatively simple to make and decorate. More cakes you might like to make through the year are specials for Christmas, New Year's Eve, Easter and that other perennial problem – the birthday cake.

I find family and friends enjoy an occasional oriental menu. Try the Chinese menu, with egg noodle soup to start and canned lychees to end it. The soup is just chicken broth made with stock cubes, thin ribbon noodles cooked in it, and at the last moment, seasoned raw beaten egg poured in through a sieve. Prawn crackers can be bought by the packet, soy sauce by the bottle. Beansprouts, water chestnuts and also bamboo shoots come in convenient sized cans. Fluffy freshly boiled rice looks very appetising combined with a pack of mixed frozen vegetables, very quickly cooked. Press lightly into a bowl, then unmould on a warm serving plate. Sprinkle with chopped cress, to make Celestial rice.

The Indian menu suits all tastes as the curry is mild. I cook equal amounts of white long grain rice and saffron rice (see page 93) for colour contrast. Poppadums, which come spiced or plain in packets, are easily fried in a small pan. Arrange a 'Party Susan' dish of different accompaniments for your curry.

Wedding buffet (pages 102–105): salami sausage rolls, cider-glazed savarin, wedding cake, stuffed olive pinwheels, festive punch and tipsy fruit salad.

Irish Christmas cake

Preparation time 15 minutes plus soaking time for dried fruit
Cooking time about 1½ hours

IMPERIAL/METRIC	AMERICAN
6 oz./175 g. sultanas	1 cup seedless white raisins
4 oz./100 g. currants	⅔ cup currants
4 oz./100 g. seedless raisins	⅔ cup seedless raisins
4 oz./100 g. glacé cherries, halved	½ cup halved candied cherries
4 oz./100 g. dark brown sugar	½ cup dark brown sugar
4 tablespoons Irish whiskey	⅓ cup Irish whiskey
4 tablespoons strained cold tea	⅓ cup strained cold tea
4 oz./100 g. butter	½ cup butter
1 tablespoon black treacle	1 tablespoon molasses
4 oz./100 g. plain flour	2 cups all-purpose flour sifted with 1 teaspoon baking powder
4 oz./100 g. self-raising flour	
1 teaspoon ground mixed spice	1 teaspoon ground mixed spice
2 eggs, beaten	2 eggs, beaten

Soak the sultanas, currants, raisins, cherries and sugar in the whiskey and tea overnight. Put the butter and treacle into a saucepan and melt them gently. Pour in the soaked fruits and liquid, stir well and take off the heat. Sieve together the flours and spice into a bowl and stir in the fruit and eggs. Turn the mixture into a greased and lined 8-inch (20-cm.) cake tin and bake in the centre of a moderate oven (350°F., 180°C., Gas Mark 4) for about 1½ hours, protecting the top of the cake if necessary with a sheet of foil to prevent overbrowning.

Allow to cool for 15 minutes in the tin and then turn out and cool. Keep in an airtight tin for at least 6 weeks before covering with almond paste and icing.

Black bun for Hogmanay

Preparation time 30 minutes
Cooking time 3–3½ hours

IMPERIAL/METRIC	AMERICAN
10 oz./275 g. plain flour	2½ cups all-purpose flour
pinch salt	pinch salt
5 oz./150 g. butter	½ cup plus 2 tablespoons butter
water to mix	water to mix
1 egg, lightly beaten	1 egg, lightly beaten
filling	**filling**
1 lb./450 g. seedless or stoned raisins	3 cups seedless or pitted raisins
1 lb./450 g. sultanas	3 cups seedless white raisins
1 lb./450 g. currants	3 cups currants
4 oz./100 g. almonds, chopped	1 cup chopped almonds
4 oz./100 g. dark brown sugar	½ cup dark brown sugar
1 tablespoon finely grated orange zest	1 tablespoon finely grated orange zest
8 oz./225 g. plain flour	2 cups all-purpose flour
1 tablespoon ground mixed spices	1 tablespoon ground mixed spices
1 teaspoon cream of tartar	1 teaspoon cream of tartar
1 teaspoon bicarbonate of soda	1 teaspoon baking soda
2 eggs, beaten	2 eggs, beaten
¼ pint/1½ dl. Scotch whisky	⅔ cup Scotch whisky
about 3 tablespoons milk	about ¼ cup milk

To make the pastry, sieve the flour and salt into a bowl. Rub in the butter and add sufficient cold water to make a firm dough. Knead lightly and roll out two-thirds of the pastry to a round about 16 inches (41 cm.) in diameter. Use this to line a greased 8–8½-inch (20–22-cm.) cake tin, easing in the fullness on the sides. Do not trim off excess pastry but allow this to lie over the sides of the cake tin.

To make the filling, place the dried fruit, almonds, sugar and orange zest in a mixing bowl. Sieve together the flour, spices, cream of tartar and bicarbonate of soda and mix into the fruit. Beat together the eggs and whisky, pour into the bowl. Add sufficient milk to just moisten the whole mixture. Pack the filling into the pastry case and then fold down the excess pastry from the sides over the filling.

Roll out the remaining pastry and use to make a neat lid, just to fit the cake tin. Brush the edges of the pastry well with beaten egg, place on the lid and seal together firmly. Prick the top of the pastry all over, brush with beaten egg and place in a moderate oven (350°F., 180°C., Gas Mark 4) for about 3–3½ hours. Protect the top of the 'bun' with a sheet of foil or brown paper to prevent overbrowning of the pastry. Cool and store in an airtight tin for weeks or preferably months before required, to allow the cake to mature.

Welsh bara brith

Preparation time 20 minutes plus rising time
Cooking time 50–60 minutes

IMPERIAL/METRIC	AMERICAN
8 oz./225 g. plain flour	2 cups all-purpose flour
½ oz./15 g. fresh yeast	½ cake compressed yeast
6 tablespoons warm water	½ cup warm water
½ teaspoon sugar	½ teaspoon sugar
½ teaspoon salt	½ teaspoon salt
½ teaspoon mixed spice	½ teaspoon mixed spice
1½ oz./40 g. butter	3 tablespoons butter
1½ oz./40 g. soft brown sugar	3 tablespoons soft brown sugar
4 oz./100 g. currants	⅔ cup currants
4 oz./100 g. sultanas	⅔ cup seedless white raisins
2 oz./50 g. candied peel, chopped	⅓ cup chopped candied peel
1 egg	1 egg
1 teaspoon clear honey	1 teaspoon clear honey

To make the yeast liquid, place 2½ oz. (65 g., ½ cup plus 2 tablespoons) flour in a large warm mixing bowl and add the chopped yeast, water and sugar. Combine well together and leave in a warm place for about 10 minutes, until frothy. Meanwhile, sieve the remaining flour with the salt and spice and rub in the butter. Stir in the brown sugar, fruit and peel and mix with the yeast liquid and the egg. Turn the dough on to a floured board and knead thoroughly. Place in a greased polythene bag and allow to rise in a warm place until doubled in bulk. Knock out the air bubbles with your knuckles, knead again and place in a greased 1-lb. (½-kg.) loaf tin. Cover again with greased polythene and allow to rise until the dough is about an inch above the sides of the tin. Remove the polythene and bake the loaf in a moderate oven (350°F., 180°C., Gas Mark 4) for 50–60 minutes. When cooked, remove from the oven and brush the top of the loaf with a little clear honey. Serve sliced with butter.

Mothering Sunday cake

Preparation time 20 minutes
Cooking time 15 minutes

IMPERIAL/METRIC	AMERICAN
4 oz./100 g. butter	½ cup butter
4 oz./100 g. castor sugar	½ cup sugar
2 eggs, lightly beaten	2 eggs, lightly beaten
4 oz./100 g. self-raising flour	1 cup all-purpose flour sifted with 1 teaspoon baking powder
pinch salt	pinch salt
2 oz./50 g. ground almonds	½ cup ground almonds
½ teaspoon almond essence	½ teaspoon almond extract
filling and icing	**filling and icing**
8 oz./225 g. butter	1 cup butter
few drops almond essence	few drops almond extract
12–15 oz./350–425 g. icing sugar, sieved	2⅔–3¼ cups sifted confectioners' sugar
few crystallised violets	few crystallized violets

Cream together the butter and sugar until light and fluffy. Gradually add the eggs, beating all the time. Fold in the dry ingredients and almond essence. Place the mixture in a well-greased Swiss roll tin approximately 12 × 9 inches (31 × 23 cm.) and bake in a moderately hot oven (375°F., 190°C., Gas Mark 5) for about 15 minutes. Turn out, cool on a wire rack and trim the edges while the cake is still warm.

To make the filling and icing, beat the butter until smooth and creamy and gradually beat in the essence and icing sugar. Slice the cake into three sections each approximately 4 × 3 inches (10 × 7·5 cm.) and sandwich them together with some of the icing. Use the remaining icing to coat the sides and top of the cake and pipe shells around the top edges. Decorate with a few crystallised violets.

Galway fish pie for Good Friday

Preparation time 15–20 minutes
Cooking time about 45 minutes
Serves 4

IMPERIAL/METRIC	AMERICAN
1 lb./450 g. fresh haddock or cod fillet	1 lb. fresh haddock or cod fillet
¼ pint/1½ dl. water	⅔ cup water
6 oz./175 g. butter	¾ cup butter
¼ pint/1½ dl. milk	⅔ cup milk
1 oz./25 g. flour	¼ cup all-purpose flour
salt and pepper to taste	salt and pepper to taste
1 teaspoon made mustard	1 teaspoon prepared mustard
2 oz./50 g. Cheddar cheese, grated	½ cup grated Cheddar cheese
1½ lb./¾ kg. potatoes	1½ lb. potatoes
2–3 tablespoons milk	3–4 tablespoons milk

Remove the skin from the fish. Rinse and drain the fish, then put into a saucepan with the measured water and half the butter. Cover and cook gently for 7–10 minutes, until the fish flakes easily. Lift the fish from the liquid and place in a buttered pie dish.

Make up the fish liquid to ½ pint (3 dl., 1¼ cups) with milk and pour this back into the saucepan. Whisk in the flour and bring to the boil, stirring constantly, until smooth and thick. Add the seasoning, mustard and cheese and mix with the fish. Cut the potatoes into small pieces, place in a saucepan, just cover with water and add salt. Cover the pan and boil for about 10 minutes, until the potatoes are tender. Strain and put the pan back over a low heat, without a lid, to dry off the potatoes. Mash them, mix in remaining butter, seasoning and add enough milk to make them soft and smooth. Fork the potato over the fish mixture and bake in the oven (400°F., 200°C., Gas Mark 6) for about 25 minutes.

Rich Easter cake

Preparation time 30 minutes
Cooking time 2½ hours

IMPERIAL/METRIC	AMERICAN
2 (8-oz./225-g.) packets almond paste	2 (½-lb.) packages almond paste
6 oz./175 g. butter	¾ cup butter
6 oz./175 g. soft brown sugar	¾ cup soft brown sugar
3 eggs, beaten	3 eggs, beaten
8 oz./225 g. self-raising flour	2 cups all-purpose flour with 2 teaspoons baking powder
1 teaspoon mixed spice	1 teaspoon mixed spice
4 oz./100 g. sultanas	⅔ cup seedless white raisins
6 oz./175 g. currants	1 cup currants
4 oz./100 g. mixed peel, chopped	⅔ cup chopped mixed peel
4 oz./100 g. mixed glacé fruits, chopped	½ cup chopped mixed candied fruits
2 tablespoons sweet sherry	3 tablespoons sweet sherry
1 tablespoon sieved apricot jam	1 tablespoon sieved apricot jam or jelly

Divide the almond paste into two parts, one slightly larger than the other. Pat into two balls, dust with sugar and allow to stand.

Cream the butter and sugar until light and fluffy. Gradually beat in the eggs, a little at a time. Fold in the dry ingredients then stir in the sultanas, currants, chopped peel, glacé fruits and finally the sherry. Place half the cake mixture in a greased and lined 7-inch (18-cm.) cake tin and smooth the top. Roll out the smaller piece of almond paste to fit the base of the cake tin and place on top of the cake mixture. Cover this with the remaining cake mixture. Smooth the top and bake in a moderate oven (350°F., 180°C., Gas Mark 4) for about 2½ hours.

Cool the cake on a wire tray and strip off the lining paper. Roll out the second portion of almond paste and cut a circle to fit the top of the cake. Brush the top of the cake with warmed apricot jam, press the almond paste circle on top and crimp the edges. Use the trimmings to make 11 small round balls and place these evenly spaced round the top of the cake. Decorate further with a fluffy chick or Easter 'eggs'.

Birthday butterfly

Preparation time 10–15 minutes plus time to assemble cake
Cooking time 40–45 minutes

IMPERIAL/METRIC	AMERICAN
7½ oz./215 g. plain flour	1¾ cups plus 2 tablespoons all-purpose flour
1½ oz. /40 g. cornflour	6 tablespoons cornstarch
3 teaspoons baking powder	3 teaspoons baking powder
¾ teaspoon salt	¾ teaspoon salt
7½ oz./215 g. castor sugar	1 cup minus 1 tablespoon sugar
3 eggs	3 eggs
generous ¼ pint/1½ dl. corn oil	generous ⅔ cup corn oil
generous ¼ pint/1½ dl. water	generous ⅔ cup water
2 oz./50 g. almond paste	2 oz. almond paste
1 tablespoon apricot jam, sieved	1 tablespoon apricot jam, sieved
1 tablespoon chocolate vermicelli	1 tablespoon chocolate vermicelli
1 red jelly sweet	1 red jelly candy
2 cloves	2 cloves
2 6-inch (15-cm.) lengths florists' wire	2 6-inch lengths thin wire
glacé icing	**glacé icing**
1½ lb./700 g. sieved icing sugar	5¼ cups sifted confectioners' sugar
1 tablespoon drinking chocolate	1 tablespoon sweetened cocoa powder

Line the base of an 8-inch (20-cm.) square cake tin with greaseproof paper and grease lightly. Sieve the dry ingredients into a bowl. Separate the egg yolks from the whites. Mix together the egg yolks, corn oil and water lightly with a fork. Stir this mixture into the dry ingredients and beat well to form a smooth, slack batter. Whisk the egg whites until stiff, fold lightly into the mixture. Place the sponge mixture in the prepared tin and bake in the centre of a moderately hot oven (375°F., 190°C., Gas Mark 5) for 40–45 minutes, until well risen and golden brown. Cool on a wire rack.

To decorate, cut the cake in half diagonally, and cut off the two opposite corners parallel with the cut. Turn the triangles of cake round so that the two short cuts come together where the body will be. Cut out two small triangles half way up the long straight edges of the 'wings' to make a classic butterfly shape.

Reserve 2 tablespoons icing sugar and add sufficient water to the remaining icing sugar to give a coating consistency. Blend the 2 tablespoons of icing sugar with the drinking chocolate dissolved in about a tablespoon of boiling water. Put the chocolate icing into a paper piping bag without cutting off the end. Coat one wing with white glacé icing. Immediately snip the end off the bag and pipe lines parallel to the long edge 1 inch (2·5 cm.) apart, then draw a skewer across them radiating out from the narrow edge of the body to the wing tip. Now ice the other wing.

When both wings are set, roll the piece of almond paste in the apricot jam and the vermicelli. Place the wings together on a cake board and put the almond paste body in the centre to cover the join. Push the cloves into the sweet and press lightly in place at the top of the body. Bend the pieces of wire into the shape of antennae and thrust through the sweet, to skewer it firmly to the cake. Press the appropriate number of candle holders down into the cake board round the outer edge.

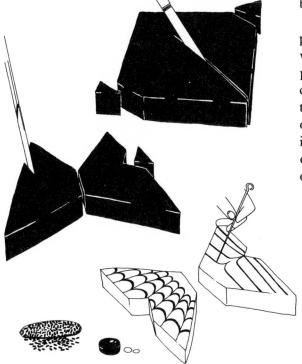

Wedding buffet

Wedding cake

*Preparation time for cake – 30 minutes, almond paste –
10 minutes, fondant icing – 15 minutes
Cooking time $3\frac{1}{2}$–$4\frac{1}{2}$ hours*

IMPERIAL/METRIC	AMERICAN
1 lb./450 g. butter	2 cups butter
1 lb./450 g. soft brown sugar	2 cups soft brown sugar
2 tablespoons black treacle	3 tablespoons molasses
9 eggs	9 eggs
1 lb. 3 oz./525 g. plain flour	$4\frac{3}{4}$ cups all-purpose flour
$2\frac{1}{2}$ teaspoons mixed spice	$2\frac{1}{2}$ teaspoons mixed spice
$1\frac{1}{2}$ teaspoons nutmeg	$1\frac{1}{2}$ teaspoons nutmeg
grated rind of 2 lemons	grated rind of 2 lemons
grated rind of 1 orange	grated rind of 1 orange
4 oz./100 g. ground almonds	1 cup ground almonds
7 oz./200 g. mixed cut candied peel	$1\frac{1}{4}$ cups mixed cut candied peel
7 oz./200 g. almonds, chopped	$1\frac{3}{4}$ cups chopped almonds
7 oz./200 g. glacé cherries, halved	scant cup halved candied cherries
9 oz./250 g. stoned raisins	$1\frac{1}{2}$ cups pitted raisins
1 lb. 3 oz./525 g. sultanas	$3\frac{1}{2}$ cups seedless white raisins
1 lb. 12 oz./800 g. currants	5 cups currants
4 tablespoons brandy	5 tablespoons brandy
apricot jam	apricot jam
egg white to brush	egg white to brush
almond paste	**almond paste**
1 lb./450 g. icing sugar	$3\frac{1}{2}$ cups sifted confectioners' sugar
2 lb./900 g. ground almonds	8 cups ground almonds
1 lb./450 g. castor sugar	2 cups sugar
4 teaspoons lemon juice	4 teaspoons lemon juice
1 teaspoon almond essence	1 teaspoon almond extract
4 eggs	4 eggs
fondant icing	**fondant icing**
1 lb. 8 oz./675 g. icing sugar	$5\frac{1}{4}$ cups sifted confectioners' sugar
2 egg whites	2 egg whites
2 tablespoons liquid glucose	3 tablespoons liquid glucose

Cream the butter and sugar together until light and fluffy. Beat in the treacle. Add the eggs, one at a time, adding a little flour with each egg after the first.

Fold in the remaining ingredients, until well mixed. Place the mixture in a 12-inch (30-cm.) square cake tin which has been greased and lined with double greaseproof paper. Smooth the surface with the back of a wet metal spoon. Protect the outside of the tin with newspaper. Bake in a preheated cool oven (275°F., 140°C., Gas Mark 1). After the first 3 hours, check at $\frac{1}{2}$ hourly intervals, using a skewer. If it comes out of the cake clean, and the cake is firm to the touch, it is cooked. Leave the cake in the tin for 15 minutes. When cool, wrap in foil and store in an airtight tin.

To make the almond paste, sift the icing sugar into a bowl, add the ground almonds and castor sugar. Stir in the lemon juice, almond essence and enough beaten egg to mix into a dry paste. Knead together with the fingers. Turn out on to a board dusted with icing sugar and knead until smooth.

Brush the top and sides of cake with boiled, sieved apricot jam. Roll out a third of the almond paste to a 12-inch (30-cm.) square and place on top of the cake. Trim edges. Roll out the remaining two thirds of the almond paste into strips the exact length and depth of the sides of the cake. Attach to the sides of the cake, joining the edges together. Leave for 1–3 days to allow the almond paste to dry before icing.

For fondant icing, place all the ingredients in a mixing bowl and blend together with a palette knife until evenly mixed. Knead together with the fingertips to form a ball. Turn out on to a board, well dusted with icing sugar, and knead until smooth and pliable. If too soft, work in a little more icing sugar. Roll out to 2 inches (5 cm.) larger than the top of the cake. Brush the almond paste with egg white. Place the icing on top of the cake and, using cornflour, rub quickly and evenly until the cake is covered. If any air bubbles appear, prick with a pin. Trim the icing at the bottom of the board.

The remaining icing could be coloured pink and moulded into roses to decorate the cake. Royal icing should be used to pipe a simple design using writing, shell and rose nozzles.

Stuffed olive pinwheels

Preparation time 15 minutes plus chilling time

IMPERIAL/METRIC	AMERICAN
1 large square white loaf, unsliced	1 large square white loaf, unsliced
4 oz./100 g. butter	½ cup butter
6 oz./175 g. salmon spread	6 oz. salmon spread
about 30 stuffed green olives	about 30 stuffed green olives

Trim the crust from one long side of the loaf, which should be very fresh. Butter and cut three long thin slices of soft bread parallel with the first cut. Trim off crusts. Spread each buttered slice with salmon spread. Arrange a row of stuffed olives (about 10) down one long edge of each slice. Roll the slices across the width of the bread tightly and wrap firmly in self-cling polythene film. Pack all the rolls together in a foil parcel and chill. When required, unwrap and slice into tiny pinwheel sandwiches.

Salami sausage rolls

Preparation time 15 minutes
Cooking time 15–20 minutes
Makes 24

IMPERIAL/METRIC	AMERICAN
8 oz./225 g. pork sausagemeat	½ lb. pork sausagemeat
2 oz./50 g. salami, finely chopped	¼ cup finely chopped salami
1-lb./450-g. packet frozen puff pastry	1-lb. package frozen puff paste
beaten egg to glaze	beaten egg to glaze

Mix the sausagemeat and salami together. Roll out the pastry to an oblong 24 × 6 inches (60 × 15 cm.). Divide in half lengthways.

Shape the sausagemeat mixture into two rolls 24 inches (60 cm.) long, using floured hands. Lay each roll down the centre of each pastry strip. Fold over and seal the edges. Brush with beaten egg and cut each length into 12. Slash the top of each roll.

Bake in a preheated hot oven (425°F., 220°C., Gas Mark 7) for 15–20 minutes.

Surprise eclairs

Preparation time 20 minutes
Cooking time 25–35 minutes
Makes 14

IMPERIAL/METRIC	AMERICAN
2½ oz./65 g. plain flour	½ cup plus 2 tablespoons all-purpose flour
pinch salt	pinch salt
¼ pint/1½ dl. water	⅔ cup water
2 oz./50 g. butter	¼ cup butter
2 eggs	2 eggs
3 oz./75 g. plain chocolate	3 oz. semi-sweet chocolate
filling	**filling**
2 teaspoons coffee essence	2 teaspoons coffee extract
¼ pint/1½ dl. thick sweetened custard	⅔ cup thick sweetened custard pie filling
2 tablespoons whipped cream	3 tablespoons whipped cream

Sieve the flour and salt together. Place the water and butter in a saucepan and bring to the boil. Remove from the heat, add the flour and beat until the mixture leaves the sides of the pan clean. Cool the mixture to blood heat and beat in the eggs, one at a time. Place the choux paste in a piping bag fitted with a ½-inch (1-cm.) plain nozzle and pipe fourteen 3-inch (7·5-cm.) lengths on to a greased baking sheet. Bake in a moderately hot oven (400°F., 200°C., Gas Mark 6) for 25–35 minutes, until crisp and golden. Cool.

Beat the coffee essence into the custard, then fold in the cream until evenly blended. Carefully slit the eclairs down one side and fill with the coffee cream. Melt the chocolate in a basin over a pan of hot water, spread over the tops of the eclairs and leave to cool.

Raspberry slices

Preparation time 25 minutes
Cooking time 12 minutes
Makes 8

IMPERIAL/METRIC	AMERICAN
1 (7½-oz./215-g.) packet frozen puff pastry	1 (7½-oz.) package frozen puff paste
2 tablespoons raspberry jam	3 tablespoons raspberry jam
4 oz./100 g. frozen raspberries	scant cup frozen raspberries
6 oz./175 g. icing sugar, sieved	1⅓ cups sifted confectioners' sugar
red food colouring	red food coloring
crème pâtissière	**crème pâtissière**
1 egg	1 egg
½ oz./15 g. flour	2 tablespoons flour
1 oz./25 g. castor sugar	2 tablespoons sugar
¼ pint/1½ dl. milk	⅔ cup milk
½ oz./15 g. butter	1 tablespoon butter
few drops vanilla essence	few drops vanilla extract

Roll out the pastry and cut into two strips, each 3 × 12 inches (7·5 × 31 cm.). Place the strips on a dampened baking sheet and bake in a hot oven (425°F., 220°C., Gas Mark 7) for 12 minutes, or until risen. Cool.

Meanwhile, make the crème pâtissière. Beat together the egg, flour and sugar. Heat the milk to boiling point then pour on to the flour mixture, beating well. Return the mixture to the pan and bring to the boil, stirring constantly, until the mixture thickens. Remove from the heat and beat in the butter and vanilla essence. Cool.

Mix together the jam and defrosted raspberries. Add sufficient water to the icing sugar to give a coating consistency and colour pink with red food colouring. Turn one pastry slice upside down and spoon over the icing. Spread the remaining pastry slice with the raspberry and jam mixture and top this with the crème pâtissière. Place the iced pastry slice on top and cut into 8 slices.

Cider-glazed savarin

Preparation time 25 minutes plus rising time
Cooking time about 25 minutes
Serves 8–10

IMPERIAL/METRIC	AMERICAN
¾ oz./20 g. fresh yeast	¾ cake compressed yeast
9 tablespoons warm milk	generous ⅔ cup warm milk
12 oz./350 g. plain flour	3 cups all-purpose flour
½ teaspoon salt	½ teaspoon salt
1½ oz./40 g. castor sugar	3 tablespoons sugar
6 oz./175 g. butter, softened	¾ cup softened butter
6 eggs, beaten	6 eggs, beaten
1 pint/6 dl. medium sweet cider	2½ cups apple cider
6 tablespoons clear honey	½ cup clear honey
icing sugar	confectioners' sugar
white and black grapes	white and purple grapes

Blend the yeast, milk and 3 oz. (75 g., ¾ cup) of the flour together until smooth. Leave to stand in a warm place until frothy. Add the remaining flour, salt, castor sugar, butter and eggs, and beat with the hand until smooth – about 4 minutes. Turn the mixture into a 9–10-inch (23–26-cm.) greased savarin or ring mould, cover with greased polythene and leave in a warm place for about 20 minutes, or until mould is about two-thirds full. Bake in the oven (400°F., 200°C., Gas Mark 6) for 20–25 minutes. Turn out.

Meanwhile, to make the syrup, place the cider in a saucepan, bring to the boil and boil steadily until reduced to half the volume. Remove from the heat, stir in the honey and cool. Prick the cooked savarin with a fine skewer and gradually pour over the cider syrup. Place the savarin on a dish, dredge with icing sugar and decorate with halved grapes.

Festive punch

Preparation time 5 minutes
Serves 40

IMPERIAL/METRIC	AMERICAN
3 gallons/14 litres dry cider	4 gallons dry apple wine
½ bottle sherry	½ bottle sherry
¼ bottle brandy	¼ bottle brandy
2 pints/generous litre soda water	5 cups soda water
orange and cucumber slices	orange and cucumber slices

Pour the cider into a punch bowl. Add the sherry and brandy. Pour in the soda water just before serving. Stir well and add the slices of orange and cucumber.

Tipsy fruit salad

Preparation time 20 minutes plus cooling time
Cooking time about 15 minutes
Serves 6–8

IMPERIAL/METRIC	AMERICAN
1½ pints/scant litre medium sweet cider	3¾ cups apple cider
3 oz./75 g. castor sugar	6 tablespoons sugar
juice of 1 lemon	juice of 1 lemon
6 oz./175 g. black grapes	⅓ lb. purple grapes
6 oz./175 g. white grapes	⅓ lb. white grapes
2 red eating apples	2 red eating apples
8 oz./225 g. strawberries	½ lb. strawberries
2 peaches	2 peaches
2 large bananas	2 large bananas

Put the cider in a large saucepan, bring to the boil and boil steadily until reduced to ¾ pint (½ litre, 2 cups), takes about 15 minutes. Stir in the sugar and lemon juice and leave until cold.

Halve and seed the grapes, core and slice the apples, hull the strawberries and stone and slice the peaches. Place these in a serving bowl, add the cold cider syrup and mix well. Just before serving, stir in the sliced bananas.

Liqueur fruit baskets

Preparation time 20 minutes
Cooking time 10 minutes
Makes 9–10

IMPERIAL/METRIC	AMERICAN
2 oz./50 g. butter	¼ cup butter
2 oz./50 g. castor sugar	¼ cup sugar
pinch salt	pinch salt
3 oz./75 g. self-raising flour	¾ cup all-purpose flour sifted with ¾ teaspoon baking powder
1 egg, beaten	1 egg, beaten
2 teaspoons milk	2 teaspoons milk
1 (8-oz./225-g.) can apricot halves	1 (8-oz.) can apricot halves
1 teaspoon arrowroot	1 teaspoon arrowroot flour
1 tablespoon apricot brandy or Cointreau	1 tablespoon apricot brandy or Cointreau
1 4-inch (10-cm.) piece angelica	1 4-inch piece angelica
2 oz./50 g. unsalted butter	¼ cup sweet butter
3 oz./75 g. icing sugar, sieved	¾ cup sifted confectioners' sugar

Cream the butter and sugar until light and fluffy. Sieve the salt and flour together. Beat the egg into the creamed mixture with a little flour, then beat in the milk, alternately with the rest of the flour. Divide the mixture between 9 or 10 well greased bun tins and bake in a moderately hot oven (400°F., 200°C., Gas Mark 6) for 10 minutes. Turn out and cool on a wire rack.

Drain the syrup from the apricots. Moisten the arrowroot with a little cold syrup and place the remainder of the syrup in a saucepan. Bring to the boil, stir in the liqueur and the moistened arrowroot.

Cook until clear. Soak the angelica to remove the crystallised sugar, cut into narrow strips and bend each into a handle shape. Beat together the unsalted butter and icing sugar. Spread a little buttercream on top of each cake, arrange an apricot half, cut side downwards, on top and spoon over the liqueur syrup. Make two cuts at opposite sides of the cake tops with the tip of a knife and press in the ends of the 'handles'. Pipe remaining buttercream in rosettes round edges.
Variation Canned cherries can be used (carefully stoned) and Kirsch instead of apricot brandy, or canned peach slices with peach brandy.

Chinese menu

Chinatown chicken

Preparation time 15–20 minutes
Cooking time about 50 minutes
Serves 4

IMPERIAL/METRIC	AMERICAN
1 chicken stock cube	1 chicken bouillon cube
¾ pint/½ litre boiling water	2 cups boiling water
4 chicken thigh portions	4 chicken thigh pieces
2 teaspoons seasoned cornflour	2 teaspoons seasoned cornstarch
1 green pepper	1 green sweet pepper
oil for frying	oil for frying
4 oz./100 g. mushrooms, sliced	1 cup sliced mushrooms
2 medium tomatoes	2 medium tomatoes
8 oz./225 g. pineapple cubes	8 oz. pineapple cubes
2 teaspoons soy sauce	2 teaspoons soy sauce

Make up the stock cube with the boiling water and use to poach the chicken portions for about 20 minutes, until tender. Remove from the heat, cool then bone the portions. Dice flesh and coat in cornflour.

Deseed and slice the green pepper. Heat 2 tablespoons oil and use to fry the mushrooms and pepper slices until the pepper is softened. Remove from the pan, place on a hot serving dish and keep hot. Add a further tablespoon of oil to the pan and use to sauté the coated chicken pieces until light golden brown.

Drain and remove the chicken pieces. Place on the serving dish with the green pepper mixture. Add the tomato quarters to the frying pan and cook until soft. Drain, place also on the serving dish. Heat the drained pineapple cubes in the frying pan and then add them to the other ingredients. Add the poaching liquid and soy sauce to the frying pan with 2 tablespoons pineapple juice. Stir over high heat to reduce and thicken slightly, then strain over the mixture.

Oriental vegetables

Preparation time 10 minutes
Cooking time 15 minutes
Serves 4

IMPERIAL/METRIC	AMERICAN
1 (8-oz./225-g.) can beansprouts	1 (8-oz.) can beansprouts
1 (8-oz./225-g.) can water chestnuts	1 (8-oz.) can water chestnuts
1 (8-oz./225-g.) can bamboo shoots	1 (8-oz.) can bamboo shoots
1 chicken stock cube	1 chicken bouillon cube
¼ teaspoon ground ginger	¼ teaspoon ground ginger
2 teaspoons cornflour	2 teaspoons cornstarch

Drain the vegetables, reserving liquid from the cans. Quarter the water chestnuts and slice the bamboo shoots thinly. Make up the liquid from the cans to ½ pint (3 dl., 1¼ cups) with water and the stock cube. Place in a saucepan, add the ginger and bring to boiling point. Moisten the cornflour with a little cold water, stir into the pan and cook until the sauce is thickened and clear. Heat the vegetables through in the sauce.

Indian menu

Mild lamb curry
White and saffron rice (see page 93)
Fried poppadums
Curry accompaniments
Melon balls with sliced mangos
Tea made with Earl Grey mixture

Mild lamb curry

Preparation time 15 minutes
Cooking time about 35 minutes
Serves 4

IMPERIAL/METRIC	AMERICAN
¼ pint/1½ dl. boiling water	⅔ cup boiling water
1 tablespoon desiccated coconut	1 tablespoon shredded coconut
1 (5-oz./150-g.) can pimentos	1 (5-oz.) can pimientos
1 tablespoon oil	1 tablespoon oil
1 onion, chopped	1 onion, chopped
1½ lb./700 g. cooked lamb, diced	1½ lb. cooked lamb, diced
1 tablespoon curry powder	1 tablespoon curry powder
2 teaspoons flour	2 teaspoons flour
½ teaspoon sugar	½ teaspoon sugar
1 tablespoon tomato purée	1 tablespoon tomato paste
salt to taste	salt to taste
8 oz./225 g. long grain rice	generous cup long grain rice
4 fried poppadums (see method)	4 fried poppadums (see method)

Pour the boiling water over the coconut and allow to stand as long as possible. Drain and dice the pimentos, reserving the liquid from the can. Heat the oil and use to fry the onion until softened and pale golden. Add the lamb and pimento and cook for 1 minute. Stir in the curry powder and flour, cook for several minutes, stirring frequently. Strain in the water from the coconut, the pimento liquid, sugar, tomato purée and about a teaspoon salt. Stir well and bring to the boil, stirring constantly. Cover and simmer for 20 minutes.

Meanwhile, cook the rice in boiling salted water – method according to the packet instructions if pre-cooked rice. When fluffy and tender, spread on a warm serving dish. Test and adjust seasoning of curry if needed. Serve in individual dishes, spooning curry into a ring of rice, and top each with a fried poppadum.

Fry each poppadum separately straight from the packet, in shallow very hot oil in a small frying pan. Hold flat with a slice, turning after a few seconds and frying for the same length of time on the other side. Drain well on soft kitchen paper.

CURRY ACCOMPANIMENTS

Mango chutney
Lime pickle
Sliced raw mild onion
Sliced banana in lemon juice
Tenderised grated coconut
Salted peanuts
Cucumber in yogurt with chopped mint

Wine service and cookery

Using a little expertise in the service of wine makes a great deal of difference to the drinking. An undistinguished white wine correctly served chilled, in a long-stemmed glass, from a bottle that has been only just opened, may meet with cries of approval. A much more expensive one, served warm in a short-stemmed glass which compels you to clutch it by the bowl in your hot hand, has little 'nose' and tastes flat and unattractive. Try not to open a good bottle several hours beforehand to use some in cooking, there will be little bouquet and fruitiness left in the wine. That's where re-bottled leftovers and big bottles of *vin ordinaire* prove so useful! The moral is, serve white and rosé wines chilled, in glasses with a stem which keeps hot convivial hands at bay; keep young red wines at room temperature having opened the bottle long in advance to allow the wine to breathe, open mature red wine only shortly before drinking. The right temperature for all red wines is 'chambré' but it does nothing for the wine to hasten matters by plunging the bottle into hot water or placing it near a fire.

Sparkling white wines seem a natural choice for any festive occasion but with the soaring price of champagne, choose from agreeable alternatives; French wines such as Veuve du Vernay or Vouvray are described as *mousseux*, the vivacious Italian Asti Spumante, or a fruity, elegant German Sekt – Rhine wines in the category of Kupferburg Gold Dry.

Use of ice in drinks

Ice may be put directly into mixed drinks or punch, but never into glasses of table wine. A little ice goes a long way if you half fill a bucket with crushed ice and force the bottles down nearly to the bottom, so that the level of ice rises up almost to the necks. Look in the yellow pages of a telephone directory to see names of suppliers of ice for parties. The off-licence should hire or supply free on loan sufficient glasses for the party and sell you drinks on a sale-or-return basis.

Allowance of wine

It is not easy to calculate the amount of wine to allow for a large party. But it helps to remember that a standard bottle holds 26½ fl. oz. (¾ litre) and serves five glasses generously; a litre bottle holds 35 fl. oz. and serves seven glasses. The most economical wine punch should be made with a 2-litre bottle, blended with a few measures of spirit – gin, brandy, etc., and fruit juice or soda water.

Storage of wine

Wine should be stored horizontally in racks, to prevent the cork from drying out, in a cool steady temperature which does not fluctuate or rise above 70°F., (21°C.). Rather than open wine too long in advance for cooking, preserve leftovers in small bottles with a minimum air space between wine and cork to prevent oxidation. White wine leftovers keep up to a week in a refrigerator, red wine even longer if you add a spoonful of sherry, port or brandy. Both varieties can be kept for months in small polythene containers (with just sufficient headspace for expansion) in the freezer. You are more likely to have leftovers if you use large bottles of *vin ordinaire* for occasional drinking and for cooking.

Order of serving

Unless sherry is served with soup, the first wine should be a dry white to accompany the hors d'oeuvre and with fish. Serve a medium dry white or rosé with poultry and white meats such as veal, or made-up dishes in a white sauce such as a *blanquette*. Red wine is best with game and red meats. Serve sweet white wines with desserts to be followed by brandy or liqueurs with coffee.

Aperitifs and liqueurs

Since an aperitif is a French term for alcoholic drinks intended to stimulate the appetite before a meal, they are usually light and dry rather than rich and heavy. Dry sherry is preferred by most people, from Fino through Manzanilla, Montilla and Amontillado (darker in colour and not so dry as a Fino sherry). Dry and sweet vermouths are served separately, or mixed, or the former mixed with gin – a Martini. Cocktails are aperitifs mainly based on gin, mixed with other ingredients. A simple cocktail, pink gin, just requires a few drops of Angostura bitters to be added to the gin. Other aperitifs have recognisable brand names like Dubonnet. The recipe may include spices and other flavourings of vegetable origin.

Liqueurs are usually heady, powerful and sweet, intended to be drunk after a meal from tiny glasses. Most of them consist of a basis of grape spirit, sweetened with sugar and flavoured with fruit, spices or herbs. Tia Maria and Kahlua are strongly coffee flavoured, Crème de cacao tastes of chocolate; yellow and green Chartreuse, Strega and Vieille Cure are flavoured with aromatic herbs.

Cooking with wine

The dish must always be sufficiently cooked to evaporate the alcohol and allow a mellow flavour to develop. In casseroles or other slow-cooking dishes, this happens automatically. In quickly cooked dishes the wine is cooked for a short time only, but briskly to ensure full evaporation. Wine can be added as a last minute 'lift' at the end of the cooking process if it is rapidly boiled to reduce by half first.

A final hint which strikes a practical note! White wine rarely leaves a stain but red wine stains should be removed as soon as possible before they become hard to shift. If the fabric permits, stretch the stained material over a bowl, sprinkle with salt and pour boiling water through it (cool water for delicate fabrics). Wash well. Dry stains should be soaked in a strong solution of salt and water.

Unusual recipes to recall happy holidays

Holidays often introduce us to dishes we would like to try again, but like some wines they do not seem to 'travel well'. It may be that the right ingredients are not available at home or that some trick in the preparation of the dish has not been passed on by the local expert.

In this chapter I have chosen some of the less familiar recipes for you to try. First, you will see my suggestion for a continental buffet party.

Of course one expects in Germany to be offered sauerkraut with a selection of the pork butcher specialities. If you compose a menu for guests with such a typically German recipe and do not want to be involved in too long a kitchen session, buy a gâteau from a continental pastry shop for the sweet.

Greece produces moussaka, the best of all savoury dishes, from minced raw lamb or cold cooked lamb. I think you will enjoy this new recipe for moussaka, with a cheese topping based on yogurt. Baclava, the Greek honey pastry, can often be bought in delicatessen shops. Always make yourself the recipes which are easiest to achieve successfully at home and supplement them with bought continental specialities.

I have chosen more unusual Italian dishes and although it may sound strange, the combination of veal and tuna is typically Italian and is a very tempting cold dish for a summer dinner party. There are also interesting dishes from France, Denmark, Spain and Holland.

Here is a tip for your future travels. If you beg the favour of a genuine recipe from a hotel keeper or chef, make sure the translation is accurate. I once misread my notes which was actually 'a little wine', as 'a litre of wine' and ended up with quite an extraordinary sauce!

Continental buffet party (pages 112–113):
mushroom salad, baked gammon in a crust, mixed
fruit flan, continental cheese dip and Edam party
cheese.

Continental buffet party

ILLUSTRATED IN COLOUR ON PAGES 110–111
This continental buffet party menu will serve about 10–12 people. If you are entertaining a larger number, include extra bowls of interesting salads and more crisps, savoury biscuits and nuts.

MENU
Continental cheese dip
Baked gammon in a crust
Edam party cheese
Mushroom salad
Mixed fruit flan

Continental cheese dip

Preparation time 10 minutes plus 2 hours marinating time

Mix together the lemon juice and seasoning and use to marinate the chopped mushrooms for 2 hours. Combine the yogurt, mayonnaise and mustard, stir in the grated cheese, mushroom mixture and finely chopped stuffed green olives. Combine all the ingredients thoroughly and chill well before serving.

IMPERIAL/METRIC	AMERICAN
1 tablespoon lemon juice	1 tablespoon lemon juice
salt and pepper to taste	salt and pepper to taste
4 oz./100 g. mushrooms, finely chopped	1 cup finely chopped mushrooms
4 tablespoons natural yogurt	$\frac{1}{3}$ cup unflavored yogurt
4 tablespoons mayonnaise	$\frac{1}{3}$ cup mayonnaise
1 teaspoon mild continental mustard	1 teaspoon mild continental mustard
4 oz./100 g. Edam cheese, grated (from whole Edam)	1 cup grated Dutch cheese (from whole cheese)
2 tablespoons finely chopped stuffed green olives or gherkins	3 tablespoons finely chopped stuffed green olives or dill pickles

Holland

Baked gammon in a crust

Preparation time 15–20 minutes plus time to soak hock
Cooking time about 2 hours 20 minutes

IMPERIAL/METRIC	AMERICAN
4 lb./1¾ kg. hock	4 lb. half ham (shank end), cured
1 pint/6 dl. beer	2½ cups beer
2 lb./1 kg. plain flour	8 cups all-purpose flour
scant 1¼ pints/7½ dl. water	3 cups water
1 tablespoon mild continental mustard	1 tablespoon mild continental mustard
2 oz./50 g. demerara sugar	¼ cup demerara sugar
cloves	cloves

Soak the hock in beer overnight or for at least 12 hours. Mix the flour and water together to form a sticky dough. Carefully mould around the joint, taking care to seal it completely. Place a wire tray over a baking tin half full of water and cover the tray with foil. Place the joint on top. Bake in a preheated hot oven (425°F., 220°C., Gas Mark 7) for 10 minutes; then reduce temperature to moderate (350°F., 180°C., Gas Mark 4) for 1½–2 hours.

Carefully remove the crust and discard. Peel off the rind from the joint and score the fat into diamond shapes. Mix the mustard with the demerara sugar, spread over the fat and stud with cloves. Return to the oven for 5–10 minutes.

Edam party cheese

Preparation time 15 minutes

IMPERIAL/METRIC	AMERICAN
1 whole Edam cheese	1 whole Edam cheese
1 (8-oz./225-g.) can pineapple cubes	1 (8-oz.) can pineapple cubes
few stuffed green olives	few stuffed green olives
about 2 tablespoons French dressing (optional)	about 3 tablespoons French dressing (optional)

Cut off the top third of the cheese, scoop out most of the centre and Vandyke the edge of the cheese. Cut the cheese into neat cubes. When ready to serve, toss together with the drained pineapple cubes, stuffed green olives and French dressing. Pile back into the cheese shell. Serve with cocktail sticks.

Use the scraps of cheese remaining to grate for the Continental cheese dip.

France

Mushroom salad

Preparation time 10 minutes
Cooking time 1 minute

IMPERIAL/METRIC	AMERICAN
8 oz./225 g. button mushrooms	2 cups button mushrooms
8 tablespoons stock	⅔ cup stock
8 tablespoons French dressing	⅔ cup French dressing
to garnish	**to garnish**
chopped parsley	chopped parsley

Slice the mushrooms and sauté in stock for 1 minute. Drain and allow to cool.

Toss in the French dressing and garnish.

Belgium

Mixed fruit flan

Preparation time 30 minutes plus chilling time
Cooking time 20–25 minutes

IMPERIAL/METRIC	AMERICAN
pâte brisee	**pâte brisee**
2 tablespoons water	3 tablespoons water
4 oz./100 g. butter, diced	½ cup butter, diced
1 egg	1 egg
8 oz./225 g. plain flour	2 cups all-purpose flour
pinch salt	pinch salt
crème pâtissière	**crème pâtissière**
2 eggs	2 eggs
1 oz./25 g. flour	¼ cup all-purpose flour
2 oz./50 g. castor sugar	¼ cup sugar
½ pint/3 dl. milk	1¼ cups milk
2 oz./50 g. butter	¼ cup butter
few drops vanilla essence	few drops vanilla extract
fruit topping	**fruit topping**
3 oranges	3 oranges
1 (8-oz./225-g.) can pineapple pieces	1 (8-oz.) can pineapple pieces
about 10 maraschino cherries	about 10 maraschino cherries
1 peach half	1 peach half
3 tablespoons apricot jam	¼ cup apricot jam
3 tablespoons juice from canned pineapple	¼ cup juice from canned pineapple

To make the pâte brisee, mix together the water, diced butter and egg. Sieve the flour and salt together, make a well in the centre and pour in the mixture. Work together lightly with the fingertips, gradually drawing in the flour. Knead lightly, form into a ball, cover and chill for 30 minutes. Roll out and use to line a 10-inch (25-cm.) flan ring. Bake blind at 375°F., 190°C., Gas Mark 5 for 20–25 minutes.

Meanwhile, make the crème pâtissière. Beat eggs, flour and sugar together. Heat the milk to boiling point and pour over the mixture, stirring well. Return the mixture to the saucepan, bring slowly just to the boil, stirring constantly, until the mixture is smooth and thick. Remove from the heat and beat in the butter and essence. Cool, pour into the flan case.

Cut the oranges into segments, removing all pith, skin and pips. Drain the pineapple pieces, maraschino cherries and peach half, if canned.

Arrange the orange segments, overlapping, round the outer edge of the flan, next arrange a ring of pineapple and finally an inner ring of cherries, leaving space for the peach half.

Put the jam into a saucepan with the juice, boil gently for 1 minute. Strain and spoon over the fruit.

Denmark

Salami salad

Preparation time 15–20 minutes
Serves 4

IMPERIAL/METRIC	AMERICAN
1 small lettuce, washed	1 small lettuce, washed
2 tablespoons mayonnaise	3 tablespoons mayonnaise
1 tablespoon lemon juice	1 tablespoon lemon juice
small bunch spring onions	small bunch scallions
2 oz./50 g. Danish blue cheese, diced	$\frac{1}{3}$ cup diced Danish blue cheese
2 oz./50 g. Samsoe cheese, diced	$\frac{1}{3}$ cup diced Samsoe cheese or similar cheese
4 small cooked potatoes, diced	4 small cooked potatoes, diced
4 oz./100 g. Danish salami	$\frac{1}{4}$ lb. Danish salami, sliced

Line a salad bowl with the lettuce leaves. Mix together the mayonnaise and lemon juice. Finely chop the spring onions and toss together with the blue cheese, Samsoe, potato and thinned mayonnaise. Reserve 8 good slices of salami, snip the rest into strips and add to the salad mixture. Place in the centre of the lined salad bowl. Cut each reserved slice of salami through from the edge to the centre, twist into a funnel shape and use to garnish the top of the salad.

Danish rolled fillets

Preparation time 20 minutes
Cooking time 10–15 minutes
Serves 4

IMPERIAL/METRIC	AMERICAN
1 lb./450 g. spinach	1 lb. spinach
salt and pepper to taste	salt and pepper to taste
2 oz./50 g. butter	$\frac{1}{4}$ cup butter
2 oz./50 g. soft breadcrumbs	1 cup soft bread crumbs
8 small plaice fillets	8 small sole fillets
4 oz./100 g. peeled prawns	$\frac{2}{3}$ cup shelled prawns or shrimp
good pinch ground nutmeg	good pinch ground nutmeg
1 egg yolk	1 egg yolk
1 lb./450 g. mashed potato	2 cups mashed potato
about $\frac{1}{4}$ pint/1$\frac{1}{2}$ dl. warm milk	about $\frac{2}{3}$ cup warm milk
$\frac{1}{4}$ pint/1$\frac{1}{2}$ dl. single cream	$\frac{2}{3}$ cup coffee cream
$\frac{3}{4}$ pint/4 dl. thick savoury white sauce	2 cups thick savory white sauce
1 tablespoon chopped parsley	1 tablespoon chopped parsley

Cook the spinach, season, chop finely and press 4 tablespoons through a sieve. Melt the butter, stir in the breadcrumbs and seasoning and stir over heat until crumbs are crisp and golden brown. Make a bed of remaining spinach in a shallow ovenproof dish.

Place the fish fillets, skin upwards, on a board and spread each with buttered crumbs. Roll up and place rolls on top of the spinach. Put a few prawns on top of each roll and season. Cover with foil and bake in a moderately hot oven (375°F., 190°C., Gas Mark 5) for 10 minutes. Meanwhile, beat the nutmeg, egg yolk and seasoning into the potato and add sufficient warm milk to make an easy piping consistency. Place the mixture in a piping bag with a large star nozzle and pipe potato round the edge of the baking dish. Stir the cream into the sauce with the sieved spinach and parsley. Reheat gently and pour over the fish.

Tivoli fruit salad

Preparation time 10 minutes
Cooking time about 5 minutes
Serves 4

IMPERIAL/METRIC	AMERICAN
1 (16-oz./450-g.) can stoned Morello cherries	1 (16-oz.) can pitted Morello cherries
1 (16-oz./450-g.) can loganberries	1 (16-oz.) can loganberries
pinch ground cinnamon	pinch ground cinnamon
1 tablespoon cornflour	1 tablespoon cornstarch
8 oz./225 g. frozen raspberries, defrosted	½ lb. frozen raspberries, defrosted
1½ oz./45 g. flaked almonds	scant ½ cup flaked almonds

Open the cans of fruit and drain the liquid off into a measuring jug. Make up to 1 pint (6 dl., 2½ cups) with water and place in a saucepan. Add the cinnamon and heat gently to boiling. Moisten the cornflour with a little cold water. Add to the pan and bring to the boil, stirring constantly, until the mixture is thick, smooth and clear. Cool and stir in the raspberries.

Put the drained canned fruit into a glass serving dish, pour over the raspberry sauce and stir gently. Cool. Just before serving, sprinkle with the almonds and serve with whipped cream.

France

Cheese talmouse

Preparation time 15–20 minutes
Cooking time 20 minutes
Makes 12

IMPERIAL/METRIC	AMERICAN
½ pint/3 dl. milk	1¼ cups milk
2½ oz./65 g. Brie, scraped	2½ oz. Brie, scraped
2 oz./50 g. butter	¼ cup butter
pinch salt	pinch salt
2 oz./50 g. flour	½ cup all-purpose flour
4 oz./100 g. curd cheese	½ cup curd cheese
3 eggs	3 eggs
6 oz./175 g. puff pastry	⅓ lb. puff paste
grated Parmesan cheese	grated Parmesan cheese

Put the milk, Brie, butter and salt into a saucepan, heat and as soon as the mixture begins to simmer, gradually add the flour. Stir with a wooden spoon for 2–3 minutes. Remove surplus moisture from the curd cheese then add to the pan and work in two of the eggs, one after the other. This paste should be the same consistency as choux pastry.

Roll out the puff pastry to ¼ inch (0·5 cm.) thickness, stamp out about 12 circles with a 2-inch (7·5-cm.) cutter and place on a greased baking sheet. Put a good teaspoonful of the Brie mixture in the centre of each pastry circle. Round the edges of the pastry circles and turn up the sides to form each into the shape of a three-cornered hat. Lightly beat the remaining egg and use this to brush the pastry cheese 'hats'. Bake in a moderately hot oven (375°F., 190°C., Gas Mark 5) for about 20 minutes until golden brown. Remove from the oven, sprinkle with Parmesan cheese and serve hot.

Normandy quiche

Preparation time 15 minutes
Cooking time 30 minutes
Serves 4

IMPERIAL/METRIC	AMERICAN
12 oz./350 g. shortcrust pastry	¾ lb. basic pie dough
1 (2-oz./50-g.) can anchovy fillets, halved	1 (2-oz.) can anchovy fillets, halved
2 rashers streaky bacon	2 bacon slices
6 oz./175 g. cooked potato, diced	¾ cup diced cooked potato
1 oz./25 g. butter	2 tablespoons butter
8 oz./225 g. onions, sliced	½ lb. onions, sliced
2 eggs	2 eggs
2 oz./50 g. Gruyère cheese	½ cup grated Gruyère cheese
salt and pepper	salt and pepper

Roll out the pastry and use to line a 9–10-inch (23–26-cm.) fluted flan ring on a baking sheet. Cover the base with a circle of foil, weight with rice or beans and bake blind in the oven (350°F., 180°C., Gas Mark 4) for 10 minutes. Remove beans and foil.

Meanwhile, drain the oil from the anchovies. Derind the bacon and cut into thin strips. Render out the fat in a frying pan. Sprinkle the bacon and diced potato over the base of the flan. Add the oil from the anchovies and butter to the bacon fat in the pan and use to fry the onion gently until limp and transparent. Beat the eggs lightly, add the onion mixture, grated cheese and seasoning to taste. Pour into the flan case, spreading carefully over the potato and bacon. Make a trellis with halved anchovy fillets over the surface and bake in the oven for 20 minutes.

Sole in brandy sauce

Preparation time 10 minutes
Cooking time 40 minutes
Serves 4

IMPERIAL/METRIC	AMERICAN
2 large sole, skinned	2 large sole, skinned
salt and pepper	salt and pepper
2 bay leaves	2 bay leaves
2 parsley sprigs	2 parsley sprigs
2 lemon slices	2 lemon slices
small bunch white grapes	small bunch white grapes
6 tablespoons double cream	½ cup heavy cream
6 tablespoons mayonnaise	½ cup mayonnaise
2 tablespoons brandy	3 tablespoons brandy

Have the sole filleted. Make a court bouillon with the bones and trimmings, simmered in salted water with the bay leaves, parsley and lemon slices for 20 minutes.

Roll up the sole fillets, skin side inwards, arrange in a buttered shallow ovenproof dish and season lightly with salt and pepper. Strain ½ pint (3 dl., 1¼ cups) of the court bouillon over the fish, cover with foil and cook in a moderately hot oven (375°F., 190°C., Gas Mark 5) for 20 minutes. Remove the foil and transfer the cooked fillets from the dish to the foil with a fish slice. Allow to cool.

Meanwhile, halve and deseed the grapes. Beat the cream into the mayonnaise, stir in the brandy, taste and adjust seasoning. Arrange the cold fillets on a serving dish, pour over the sauce and garnish with the grape halves.

Veal with vermouth sauce

Preparation time 10 minutes
Cooking time 20–25 minutes
Serves 4

IMPERIAL/METRIC	AMERICAN
4 veal escalopes	4 veal scallops
1 egg, beaten with 2 tablespoons milk	1 egg, beaten with 3 tablespoons milk
toasted breadcrumbs for coating	toasted bread crumbs for coating
2 oz./50 g. butter	¼ cup butter
2 tablespoons oil	3 tablespoons oil
1 wine glass extra dry French vermouth	1 wine glass extra dry French vermouth
sprig of rosemary	sprig of rosemary
1 (8-oz./225-g.) can tomatoes	1 (8-oz.) can tomatoes
salt and pepper	salt and pepper
8 oz./225 g. pasta bows or shells	½ lb. pasta bows or shells

Season the escalopes, turn in beaten egg and coat in breadcrumbs. Heat the butter and 1 tablespoon oil in a frying pan, use to fry the escalopes until golden brown, about 5 minutes each side. Remove and keep hot. Strain the juices into a saucepan, pour in the glass of extra dry French vermouth, add a small sprig of rosemary and the tomatoes. Season to taste. Cover the pan and cook gently for about 15 minutes. Press through a sieve.

Meanwhile, cook the pasta, drain and toss with the remaining oil. Put in a warm serving dish, arrange the escalopes on top and pour the sauce over.

Boeuf en croûte

ILLUSTRATED IN COLOUR ON PAGE 1
Preparation time 25 minutes
Cooking time about 40 minutes
Serves 6–8

IMPERIAL/METRIC	AMERICAN
filling	**filling**
½ oz./15 g. butter	1 tablespoon butter
1 small onion, chopped	1 small onion, chopped
4 oz./100 g. mushrooms, chopped	1 cup chopped mushrooms
1 oz./25 g. long grain rice, cooked	scant ¼ cup long grain rice, cooked
½ teaspoon mixed dried herbs	½ teaspoon mixed dried herbs
few drops Tabasco sauce	few drops Tabasco sauce
salt and pepper to taste	salt and pepper to taste
2-lb./1-kg. piece fillet of beef	2-lb. piece beef filet
1 tablespoon oil	1 tablespoon oil
1 lb./450 g. frozen puff pastry	1 lb. frozen puff pastry
beaten egg to glaze	beaten egg to glaze

Melt the butter and fry the chopped onion until soft, add the chopped mushrooms, cooked rice, herbs, Tabasco sauce, salt, pepper and cook for a further 5 minutes.

Trim the fillet of beef, brush with oil and place on a baking sheet in a hot oven (400°F., 200°C., Gas Mark 6) for 10 minutes to seal the meat. Cool.

Roll out the puff pastry to an oblong large enough to wrap the steak in. Reserve a little pastry for decoration. Place the cooled fillet in the centre of the pastry and cover with the cooled onion and mushroom mixture. Fold the pastry to the centre, dampen edges and seal. Turn over and seal the ends. Use the reserved pastry and any trimmings for decoration. Brush with beaten egg and bake in a hot oven (425°F., 220°C., Gas Mark 7) for about 30 minutes. The pastry should be golden brown and the meat rare. Serve with a salad or vegetables.

Germany

Maultaschen

*Preparation time 15–20 minutes plus time for
dough to rest
Cooking time 15 minutes
Serves 4*

IMPERIAL/METRIC	AMERICAN
1 white bread roll	1 white bread roll
8 oz./225 g. flour	2 cups all-purpose flour
salt to taste	salt to taste
3 eggs	3 eggs
1 oz./25 g. butter	2 tablespoons butter
1 onion, chopped	1 onion, chopped
12 oz./350 g. cooked spinach, sieved	generous 1½ cups sieved cooked spinach
10 oz./275 g. cooked lamb, minced	1¼ cups ground cooked lamb
pinch ground nutmeg	pinch ground nutmeg
2 tablespoons chopped parsley	3 tablespoons chopped parsley
1 egg white	1 egg white
2 chicken stock cubes	2 chicken bouillon cubes
1½ pints/scant litre boiling water	3¾ cups boiling water

Soak the bread roll in water. Mix together the flour, salt, 2 eggs and 2 tablespoons water to make a stiff dough. Knead lightly then allow to rest for 1 hour.

Melt the butter and use to fry the onion until soft but not coloured. Squeeze out the bread roll and crumble into the pan with the spinach, lamb, nutmeg, salt, parsley and remaining whole egg. Roll out the pastry and cut into 4-inch (10-cm.) squares with a fluted pastry wheel if possible. Divide the filling between the squares, brush the edges with egg white and seal well together. Make up the stock cubes with the boiling water and use to poach the maultaschen for about 15 minutes, until cooked. Either serve the maultaschen with the stock as a soup or drain them and sauté in melted butter until golden and serve with salad.

Sauerkraut garniert

*Preparation time 10 minutes
Cooking time 45 minutes
Serves 4*

IMPERIAL/METRIC	AMERICAN
¼ pint/1½ dl. Riesling or other dry white wine	⅔ cup Riesling or other dry white wine
4 thick slices fat streaky bacon	4 thick fat bacon slices
2 bay leaves	2 bay leaves
2 lb./1 kg. sauerkraut	2 lb. sauerkraut
2 carrots, grated	2 carrots, grated
1 oz./25 g. flour	¼ cup all-purpose flour
1 oz./25 g. butter, melted	2 tablespoons melted butter
2 teaspoons sugar	2 teaspoons sugar
4 knackwurst	4 knackwurst

Place the wine in a small saucepan with the slices of bacon and bay leaves. Bring to the boil and simmer for 10 minutes to partially cook the bacon and reduce the wine. Remove the bacon.

Put the sauerkraut and carrot into an ovenproof casserole. Mix together the flour and melted butter until smooth. Add the strained reduced wine and the sugar and mix well. Stir this into the sauerkraut, cover and place in a moderately hot oven (400°F., 200°C., Gas Mark 6) for 5 minutes. Arrange the cooked meat and sausages on the bed of sauerkraut, cover and return to the oven for 30 minutes.

Cabbage with plum sauce

Preparation time 15 minutes
Cooking time 45 minutes
Serves 4

IMPERIAL/METRIC	AMERICAN
2 tablespoons plum jam	3 tablespoons plum jam
¼ pint/1½ dl. red wine	⅔ cup red wine
2 oz./50 g. butter	¼ cup butter
2 thick slices bacon	2 thick bacon slices
2 lb./1 kg. red cabbage, sliced	2 lb. red cabbage, sliced
1 large dessert apple, cored	1 large eating apple, cored
1 medium onion, sliced	1 medium onion, sliced
salt and pepper to taste	salt and pepper to taste

Melt the jam in the wine in a small saucepan. Use ½ oz. (15 g., 1 tablespoon) of the butter to grease a large saucepan. Arrange the bacon on the greased base of the pan, then cover with a layer of cabbage. Slice the apple and put a layer of apple and onion slices over the cabbage. Sprinkle with some of the wine mixture and season to taste. Repeat layers of cabbage, onion, apple and wine mixture, ending with a layer of cabbage and the remaining butter in knobs. Cover tightly and cook over a low heat for 45 minutes.

German hot potato salad

Preparation time 15 minutes
Cooking time 25 minutes
Serves 4–6

IMPERIAL/METRIC	AMERICAN
1 lb./½ kg. new potatoes	1 lb. new potatoes
8 rashers streaky bacon	8 bacon slices
1 lb./450 g. sausages	1 lb. sausages
2–3 tablespoons chopped onion	3–4 tablespoons chopped onion
2 tablespoons chopped celery heart	3 tablespoons chopped celery heart
2 tablespoons cider or wine vinegar	3 tablespoons cider or wine vinegar
4 tablespoons water	⅓ cup water
1 teaspoon sugar	1 teaspoon sugar
½ teaspoon paprika pepper	½ teaspoon paprika pepper
1 tablespoon chopped gherkin	1 tablespoon chopped sweet dill pickles
salt and pepper	salt and pepper

Wash the unpeeled potatoes and cook in boiling salted water until just tender. Drain in a colander, then peel and slice, keeping potato slices hot under a warm teacloth.

While the potatoes are cooking, remove the rind from the bacon. Cut 2 or 3 rashers in half, roll up and secure with a skewer for the garnish. Dice the remaining bacon and fry gently until the fat runs, add the sausages and cook until they are golden brown all over. Remove and drain the sausages and bacon and keep warm. Add the onion and celery heart to the sausage fat and fry until just turning golden. Pour off any excess fat. Mix together the vinegar, water, sugar, paprika and chopped gherkin, pour into the pan and bring to the boil. Remove from the heat, carefully mix into the potatoes, add seasoning to taste and sprinkle with the cooked diced bacon. Arrange the sausages on top and garnish with grilled bacon rolls. Serve with a fresh green salad.

119

Rheinischer salat

Preparation time 10 minutes plus cooling time
Cooking time about 10 minutes
Serves 4

IMPERIAL/METRIC	AMERICAN
1 lb./½ kg. potatoes, diced	1 lb. potatoes, diced
1 chicken stock cube	1 chicken bouillon cube
2 tablespoons boiling water	3 tablespoons boiling water
7 tablespoons white wine	8 tablespoons white wine
¼ pint/1½ dl. mayonnaise	⅔ cup mayonnaise
1 tablespoon chopped chives	1 tablespoon chopped chives
8 frankfurters	8 frankfurters
8 gherkins	8 sweet dill pickles

Cook the potatoes in boiling salted water until tender but not too soft. Drain and shake gently to dry. Dissolve the stock cube in the boiling water, add the wine and pour over the potatoes while they are still warm enough to absorb it.

When cold, fold in the mayonnaise and chives.

Chill. Place the frankfurters in a saucepan of boiling water, remove from the heat, cover tightly and allow to stand for 5 minutes. Drain. Place the potato salad in a serving dish, arrange the hot frankfurters on top and garnish with gherkin fans.

Cabbage and sausage soup

Preparation time 20 minutes
Cooking time about 2 hours
Serves 4–6

IMPERIAL/METRIC	AMERICAN
1 young Savoy cabbage	1 young white cabbage
8 oz./¼ kg. pickled belly of pork	½ lb. picnic shoulder pork or salt pork
1 lb./½ kg. small carrots	1 lb. small carrots
1 lb./½ kg. small potatoes	1 lb. small potatoes
8 oz./¼ kg. onions, sliced	½ lb. onions, sliced
8 oz./¼ kg. leeks, sliced	½ lb. leeks, sliced
2 sticks celery, chopped	2 stalks celery, chopped
sprig each of parsley and thyme	sprig each of parsley and thyme
2 bay leaves	2 bay leaves
1 lb./450 g. frankfurters	1 lb. frankfurters
8 oz./225 g. broad beans	½ lb. fava or lima beans
8 oz./225 g. peas	½ lb. peas
ground black pepper	ground black pepper

Remove any coarse or discoloured leaves from the cabbage. Cook in boiling, salted water for 5 minutes and drain.

Put the belly of pork in a large saucepan, cover with cold water. Bring to the boil, cook gently for 5 minutes and discard the water. Leave the pork in the saucepan and add the carrots, potatoes, onion, leeks, celery and herbs tied in a bunch. Add 4 pints (2¼ litres, 10 cups) water, bring slowly to the boil and skim. Cover and simmer gently for 1½ hours. Chop the blanched cabbage and add to the pan with the drained sausages, beans and peas. Season with black pepper (the pickled pork usually makes salt unnecessary) and continue cooking for a further 20–30 minutes.

Remove the bunch of herbs, lift out the pork and cut into small slices. Turn the soup and frankfurters into a tureen and add the sliced pork. Alternatively, serve the frankfurters and pork, garnished with the potatoes and other vegetables as a main dish, preceded by the soup as a first course. The frankfurters and pork also make a tasty dish served cold with the drained vegetables mixed with salad dressing.

Fruit beer fritters

Preparation time 10 minutes
Cooking time about 5 minutes per fritter
Serves 4

IMPERIAL/METRIC	AMERICAN
½ pint/3 dl. beer	1¼ cups beer
6 oz./175 g. plain flour	1½ cups all-purpose flour
¼ teaspoon ground mace	¼ teaspoon ground mace
3 large cooking apples	3 large baking apples
oil for frying	oil for frying
castor sugar	sugar

Gradually beat the beer into the flour and spice until a smooth batter is formed. Allow it to stand while preparing the fruit. Peel, core and slice the apples into rings about ½ inch (1 cm.) thick. Dip each apple slice in batter and fry in hot deep oil for 3–5 minutes, until crisp and golden brown, or shallow fry for about 2½ minutes on each side. Serve hot sprinkled with sugar.

Greece

Moussaka with yogurt topping

Preparation time 20 minutes
Cooking time 50 minutes
Serves 4

IMPERIAL/METRIC	AMERICAN
3 tablespoons oil	4 tablespoons oil
12 oz./350 g. lamb, finely minced	1½ cups finely ground lamb
1 medium onion, chopped	1 medium onion, chopped
2 tablespoons tomato purée	3 tablespoons tomato paste
salt and pepper	salt and pepper
2 medium potatoes	2 medium potatoes
1 large aubergine	1 large eggplant
1 red pepper	1 red sweet pepper
1 beef stock cube	1 beef bouillon cube
¼ pint/1½ dl. boiling water	⅔ cup boiling water
1 egg, separated	1 egg, separated
1 egg yolk	1 egg yolk
2 cartons natural yogurt	2 cartons unflavored yogurt
2 oz./50 g. cheese, grated	½ cup grated cheese

Heat half the oil and use to fry the meat and onion lightly for a few minutes, until just coloured. Add the tomato purée and season well. Remove to an ovenproof dish.

Slice the potatoes and aubergine thinly, deseed and slice the pepper thinly. Add the remaining oil to the pan and use to fry the potato, aubergine and red pepper slices until softened. Spread this mixture over the meat. Make up the stock cube with the boiling water and pour into the casserole. Cover and cook in a moderately hot oven (375°F., 190°C., Gas Mark 5) for 30 minutes.

Beat the egg yolks into the yogurt, stir in the grated cheese and season to taste. Fold in the stiffly beaten egg white, spoon over the moussaka and bake uncovered for about 20 minutes, until well risen and golden brown.

Note The topping tends to sink slightly as soon as it comes out of the oven.

Pilaff with courgettes

Preparation time 15 minutes
Cooking time about 35 minutes
Serves 4

IMPERIAL/METRIC	AMERICAN
1 lb./450 g. stewing lamb, diced	1 lb. lamb stew meat, diced
seasoned flour for coating	seasoned flour for coating
3 tablespoons oil	4 tablespoons oil
1 large onion, sliced	1 large onion, sliced
2 large tomatoes, sliced	2 large tomatoes, sliced
½ teaspoon ground bay leaves	½ teaspoon ground bay leaves
salt and pepper to taste	salt and pepper to taste
6 oz./175 g. long grain rice	scant cup long grain rice
¾ pint/4 dl. boiling water	2 cups boiling water
1 tablespoon tomato purée	1 tablespoon tomato paste
¼ teaspoon ground ginger	¼ teaspoon ground ginger
1 lb./450 g. courgettes, sliced	1 lb. small zucchini, sliced

Coat the meat in seasoned flour. Heat 2 tablespoons oil and use to fry the onion and meat lightly for 3 minutes. Add the sliced tomatoes, ground bay leaves and seasoning to taste. Stir in the rice and continue cooking for a further 3 minutes. Add the boiling water, cover and simmer for 25 minutes.

Meanwhile, beat together the remaining tablespoon of oil, tomato purée, ground ginger and pepper to taste. Spoon over the courgettes in a small pan and cook covered until tender (about 10 minutes). Place in a warm shallow serving dish. When the rice has absorbed all the liquid, spoon the mixture over the courgettes and serve at once.

Holland

Dutch pasties

Preparation time 20–25 minutes
Cooking time 30 minutes
Serves 4

IMPERIAL/METRIC	AMERICAN
1 lb./450 g. sausages	1 lb. sausages
½ oz./15 g. bacon fat or butter	1 tablespoon bacon fat or butter
12 oz./350 g. cooking or dessert apples	¾ lb. baking or eating apples
about 2 tablespoons raisins or sultanas	about 3 tablespoons raisins or seedless white raisins
½ lemon	½ lemon
ground cinnamon or nutmeg to taste	ground cinnamon or nutmeg to taste
1 egg, beaten	1 egg, beaten
12 oz./350 g. shortcrust pastry using 12 oz./350 g. flour etc.	basic pie dough using 3 cups all-purpose flour etc.

Skin the sausages and fry in the hot fat until golden all over, then leave to cool. Peel, core and chop the apples, mix with the dried fruit. Sprinkle generously with lemon juice and sparingly with the ground spice, then mix well. Add sufficient beaten egg to bind.

Roll out the pastry about ¼ inch (0·5 cm.) thick and cut 8 circles about 6 inches (15 cm.) in diameter. Divide the apple filling between the circles, piling it in a semi-circle on one half of each circle. Place a sausage on top. Brush the edges of the pastry with egg and fold over in a half moon shape. Press the pastry edges firmly together and crimp by squeezing between finger and thumb into little scallops. Add a spoonful of water to the remaining egg and brush all over the pasties. Place them on a greased baking tray. Work up the pastry trimmings, roll them out and cut into narrow strips to make large initial letters for each pasty. Place in position and make a couple of little slits in each pasty for the steam to escape. Bake in a moderately hot oven (400°F., 200°C., Gas Mark 6) for about 30 minutes. Serve hot or cold.

Hungary

Paprika goulash

Preparation time 15 minutes
Cooking time 1 hour 15 minutes
Serves 4

IMPERIAL/METRIC	AMERICAN
2 tablespoons oil	3 tablespoons oil
1 large onion, chopped	1 large onion, chopped
12 oz./350 g. pie veal, diced	¾ lb. veal stew meat, diced
12 oz./350 g. pork bladebone, diced	¾ lb. pork blade steaks, diced
1 (8-oz./225-g.) can tomatoes	1 (8-oz.) can tomatoes
1 beef stock cube	1 beef bouillon cube
¼ pint/1½ dl. boiling water	⅔ cup boiling water
salt and pepper to taste	salt and pepper to taste
1 tablespoon sweet paprika pepper	1 tablespoon sweet paprika pepper
good pinch sugar	good pinch sugar
¼ pint/1½ dl. soured cream	⅔ cup sour cream

Heat the oil in a flameproof casserole and use to cook the onion until just soft. Add the meats and sauté until lightly coloured. Add the contents of the can of tomatoes, crumbled stock cube in the boiling water, seasonings and sugar. Bring to the boil, cover and cook over a gentle heat for 1¼ hours or until the meat is tender. Serve topped with soured cream and a light sprinkling of paprika.

Italy

Veal and tuna platter

Preparation time 10–15 minutes
Cooking time about 25 minutes
Serves 4

IMPERIAL/METRIC	AMERICAN
4 escalopes veal	4 veal scallops
seasoned flour	seasoned flour
1½ oz./40 g. butter	3 tablespoons butter
2 tablespoons water	3 tablespoons water
4 tablespoons white Italian vermouth	⅓ cup white Italian vermouth
1 small onion, chopped	1 small onion, chopped
2 bay leaves	2 bay leaves
1 carrot, sliced	1 carrot, sliced
salt and pepper to taste	salt and pepper to taste
¼ pint/1½ dl. double cream, whipped	⅔ cup whipping cream, whipped
2 tablespoons mayonnaise	3 tablespoons mayonnaise
1 (7-oz./200-g.) can tuna	1 (7-oz.) can tuna
to garnish	**to garnish**
1 tablespoon chopped parsley	1 tablespoon chopped parsley
paprika pepper	paprika pepper

Coat the veal lightly with the seasoned flour, fry for 3 minutes on each side in the butter. Add the water, vermouth, onion, bay leaves and carrot. Simmer, covered, until the veal is tender – about 20 minutes. Season to taste.

Remove the veal, drain well, cool on a serving dish. Strain the juices from the pan and cool. Skim off the fat and mix the juices with the whipped cream, mayonnaise and drained flaked tuna. Pound with a pestle and mortar or liquidise. Pour the sauce over the meat. Garnish with chopped parsley and a sprinkling of paprika pepper. Serve with green salad.

Venetian veal ragoût

Preparation time about 10 minutes plus marinating time
Cooking time 1 hour 30 minutes
Serves 4

IMPERIAL/METRIC	AMERICAN
¼ pint/1½ dl. white wine	⅔ cup white wine
1 tablespoon oil	1 tablespoon oil
salt and pepper to taste	salt and pepper to taste
1 teaspoon juniper berries	1 teaspoon juniper berries
2 lb./1 kg. shoulder of veal, diced	2 lb. shoulder of veal, diced
2 large onions, chopped	2 large onions, chopped
2 cloves garlic, crushed	2 cloves garlic, crushed
1 teaspoon paprika pepper	1 teaspoon paprika pepper
1 tablespoon flour	1 tablespoon flour
1 (15-oz./425-g.) can tomatoes, sieved	1 (15-oz.) can tomatoes, sieved
1 chicken stock cube	1 chicken bouillon cube
12 oz./350 g. cooked saffron rice (see page 93)	generous 2 cups cooked saffron rice (see page 93)
1 tablespoon chopped parsley	1 tablespoon chopped parsley

Make a marinade with the wine, 1 teaspoon oil, salt, pepper and the juniper berries. Pour over the veal and marinate overnight or for at least 6 hours.

Put the meat in a flameproof casserole. Heat the remaining oil and use to fry the onion and garlic, until just soft but not brown. Stir in the paprika and flour and add this mixture to the casserole, stirring well. Strain over the marinade. Add the sieved can of tomatoes and juice, crumbled stock cube and bring slowly to the boil, stirring constantly. Cover and simmer for 1½ hours.

Line a serving dish with hot saffron rice and pour veal into the centre. Sprinkle with chopped parsley.

Fresh mussel salad

Preparation time 15 minutes plus chilling time
Cooking time 10–15 minutes
Serves 4

IMPERIAL/METRIC	AMERICAN
2 pints/1 litre mussels	5 cups mussels
¼ pint/1½ dl. dry white wine	⅔ cups dry white wine
4 oz./100 g. pasta shells	1 cup pasta shells
1 tablespoon mild continental mustard	1 tablespoon mild continental mustard
¼ pint/1½ dl. mayonnaise	⅔ cup mayonnaise
4 tablespoons cooked peas	⅓ cup cooked peas
to garnish	**to garnish**
2 tablespoons chopped parsley	3 tablespoons chopped parsley

Scrub the mussels and remove the beards. Place in a heavy pan with the wine, cover tightly and shake occasionally over high heat for a few minutes, or until all the shells are open. Drain through a colander, reserving the liquid, cool and remove the mussels from their shells. Boil the liquid hard until reduced to 4 tablespoons. Strain again through a fine sieve. Meanwhile, cook the pasta shells in boiling salted water until tender. Drain and rinse in cold water.

Chill the mussels, pasta shells and the liquid separately. Combine the liquid, mustard and mayonnaise, then fold in the mussels, pasta shells and peas. Serve sprinkled with chopped parsley.

Poached pears in vermouth

Preparation time 5 minutes
Cooking time about 25 minutes
Serves 4

IMPERIAL/METRIC	AMERICAN
2 oz./50 g. sugar	¼ cup sugar
2 tablespoons redcurrant jelly	3 tablespoons red currant jelly
¼ pint/1½ dl. water	⅔ cup water
¼ pint/1½ dl. red Italian vermouth	⅔ cup red Italian vermouth
strips of lemon zest	strips of lemon zest
4 ripe pears	4 ripe pears

Dissolve the sugar and jelly in the water over gentle heat, then add the vermouth and lemon zest. Peel, halve and core the pears and place in the liquor. Add more water if the pears are not covered. Simmer until just tender. Remove the pears to a serving dish. Reduce the liquid to syrup consistency by boiling and pour over the pears. Serve chilled.

Snowstorm cassata

Preparation time 15 minutes plus freezing time
Serves 4

IMPERIAL/METRIC	AMERICAN
¾-pint/½-litre block vanilla ice cream	2 cups vanilla ice cream
¼ pint/1½ dl. double cream	⅔ cup whipping cream
1 tablespoon anise liqueur (such as Pernod)	1 tablespoon anise liqueur (such as Pernod)
2 oz./50 g. chestnut purée	2 oz. chestnut paste
4 sponge fingers	4 lady fingers

Soften the ice cream and use to line a small foil pudding basin. Refreeze this while preparing the chestnut cream. The double cream should be semi-frozen until mushy. Beat the liqueur into the chilled chestnut purée. Whip the cream and fold into the chestnut mixture. Return this mixture to the freezer for 2 hours, stirring every ½ hour. Pour into the ice cream mould and top with a layer of broken sponge fingers. Cover the cassata with foil and freeze. When required, turn out on to a serving dish.

Marsala oranges

Preparation time 15 minutes plus chilling time
Cooking time about 15 minutes
Serves 4

IMPERIAL/METRIC	AMERICAN
4 large oranges	4 large oranges
6 oz./175 g. sugar	¾ cup sugar
½ pint/3 dl. water	1¼ cups water
2 tablespoons boiling water	3 tablespoons boiling water
2 tablespoons Marsala	3 tablespoons Marsala

Grate the zest of two oranges, then peel all the oranges carefully, removing the pith. Arrange them in a serving dish. In a saucepan, dissolve the sugar in the water and then boil, without stirring, until golden coloured. Remove from the heat. Carefully, to avoid being splashed, pour in the boiling water. Return to the heat for a few seconds, stirring. Add the Marsala and grated orange zest. Allow the syrup to cool slightly and then pour over the oranges. Chill and serve the oranges sliced with syrup poured over.

Spain

Flamenco fish salad

Preparation time 15 minutes
Cooking time 20 minutes
Serves 4

IMPERIAL/METRIC	AMERICAN
12 oz./350 g. fresh cod fillet	¾ lb. fresh cod fillet
12 oz./350 g. smoked cod fillet	¾ lb. smoked cod fillet
1 (2½-oz./70-g.) can pimentos	1 (2½-oz.) can pimientos
2 tablespoons olive oil	3 tablespoons olive oil
12 oz./350 g. cooked saffron rice (see page 93)	generous 2 cups cooked saffron rice (see page 93)
salt and pepper to taste	salt and pepper to taste
1 oz./25 g. toasted flaked almonds	2 tablespoons toasted flaked almonds
12 black olives	12 ripe olives
12 stuffed green olives	12 stuffed green olives
6 gherkins	6 sweet dill pickles

Poach both kinds of fish together in unsalted water for about 20 minutes, until tender. Drain, flake and allow to cool. Beat together the liquid from the can of pimentos and the oil. Fold into the saffron rice, together with the fish. Taste and season as required. Pile up on a serving platter, sprinkle with toasted almonds and surround with piles of sliced pimento, whole black and green olives and sliced gherkins.

Note The original recipe uses salt cod, rarely available here, instead of smoked cod. If you can buy salt cod, soak overnight and rinse off with fresh water before cooking.

Gazpacho Andaluz

Preparation time 15 minutes plus chilling time
Serves 4

IMPERIAL/METRIC	AMERICAN
2 cloves garlic, crushed	2 cloves garlic, crushed
2 oz./50 g. soft white breadcrumbs	1 cup soft white bread crumbs
2 tablespoons wine vinegar	3 tablespoons wine vinegar
1 large cucumber, peeled	1 large cucumber, peeled
1 green pepper	1 green sweet pepper
1 small onion, chopped	1 small onion, chopped
5 tablespoons olive oil	6 tablespoons olive oil
2 lb./900 g. ripe tomatoes, chopped	2 lb. ripe tomatoes, chopped
salt and pepper to taste	salt and pepper to taste

Soak the garlic and breadcrumbs in the vinegar. Chop the cucumber, deseed and finely slice the green pepper. Pound together the breadcrumb mixture, onion, cucumber and pepper with a pestle and mortar, or liquidise. Whisk in the oil. Sieve the chopped tomatoes (or if not available use a 1-lb. 13-oz. (800-g.) can of tomatoes) and stir into the soup. Taste and add seasoning, a little water or vinegar to taste. Chill well before serving.

If liked, retain a few cubes of cucumber and green pepper for a garnish, or offer toast croûtons at the table for guests to add to the soup. The flavour is best developed if the soup is not only thoroughly chilled, but an ice cube added to each plate just before serving.